D-Day 1944 (2)

Utah Beach & the US Airborne Landings

Campaign • 104

D-Day 1944 (2)

Utah Beach & the US Airborne Landings

Steven J Zaloga · Illustrated by Howard Gerrard

Series editor Lee Johnson · *Consultant editor* David G Chandler

First published in Great Britain in 2004 by Osprey Publishing.
Midland House, West Way, Botley, Oxford OX2 0PH, UK
443 Park Avenue South, New York, NY 10016, USA
Email: info@ospreypublishing.com

A CIP catalog record for this book is available from the British Library

ISBN-13: 978-1-84176-365-1

Typeset in Helvetica Neue and ITC New Baskerville

Editor: Lee Johnson
Design: The Black Spot
Index by Glyn Sutcliffe
Maps by The Map Studio
3D bird's-eye views by The Black Spot
Battlescene artwork by Howard Gerrard
Origination by PPS Grasmere Ltd., Leeds, UK
Printed in China through World Print Ltd.

08 09 10 11 12 14 13 12 11 10 9 8 7 6 5

FOR A CATALOGUE OF ALL BOOKS PUBLISHED BY OSPREY PLEASE CONTACT:

NORTH AMERICA
Osprey Direct, C/o Random House Distribution Center,
400 Hahn Road, Westminster, MD 21157, USA
E-mail: info@ospreydirect.com

ALL OTHER REGIONS
Osprey Direct UK, P.O. Box 140, Wellingborough,
Northants, NN8 2FA, UK
E-mail: info@ospreydirect.co.uk

www.ospreypublishing.com

Author's Note

The author is indebted to many people who assisted on
this project and would like to thank David Isby for his help
with photos. Thanks also go to Randy Hackenburg and Jay
Graybeal of the Military History Institute at the Army War
College in Carlisle Barracks, PA (MHI); Charles Lemons and
Candace Fuller of the Patton Museum at Ft. Knox,
Kentucky; the staff of the US National Archives and
Records Administration (NARA), College Park, Maryland,
and the staff of the US Army Ordnance Museum, Aberdeen
Proving Ground (USAOM), for their help.
For brevity, the normal abbreviations for US and German
tactical units have been used here. So 1/8th Infantry
indicates the 1st Battalion, 8th Infantry Regiment while
C/8th Infantry indicates Company C, 8th Infantry Regiment.
In the German case, II./GR.919 indicates 2nd Battalion,
919th Grenadier Regiment while 2./GR.919 indicates
2nd Company, 919th Grenadier Regiment.

Artist's note

KEY TO MILITARY SYMBOLS

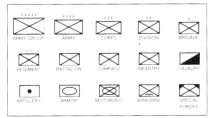

CONTENTS

On the way to Utah Beach. Task Force U sets sail for Normandy on 5 June with a flotilla of LCI (landing craft, infantry) ahead, as seen from the bridge of an LST (landing ship, tank). (NARA)

INTRODUCTION

The plans for the US Army at Utah Beach were a bold attempt to use airborne units to overcome the difficult terrain behind the beachhead. In the largest combat airdrop of the war so far, two airborne divisions were delivered at night behind enemy lines with the aim of securing the key bridges and access points. Due to the inherent risks of such a night operation, the paratroopers were very scattered and unable to carry out many of their specific missions. Yet in spite of these problems, the gamble paid off. The landings at Utah Beach were never in doubt, and within a day the US Army had a firm foothold in Normandy. The earlier book in this D-Day series on Omaha Beach[1] provides a more detailed account of the planning and preparation for US Army operations on D-Day. This book is intended to complement it by providing a more detailed look at US Army operations subsequent to D-Day. With the capture of Cherbourg and the Cotentin peninsula, the Wehrmacht lost any hope that the Allies could be dislodged from France.

THE STRATEGIC BACKGROUND

Allied planning for Operation Overlord recognized the need for extensive port facilities to supply the armies for later operations in France. The German army presumed that the Allies would conduct their invasion in the Pas de Calais where there were many excellent ports. Consequently, the main German defensive effort was concentrated in this area, making it far less attractive to Allied planners, who turned instead to Brittany and Normandy. Brittany had several excellent ports such as Brest, but the Breton peninsula was more distant from English ports than either the Pas de Calais or Normandy. In addition, had the Allies landed in Brittany, German forces might have contained their advance by sealing off the relatively narrow exit from the Breton peninsula. As a result, Brittany was dropped from consideration. The Normandy coast had few large port facilities except for Cherbourg on the Cotentin peninsula. Nevertheless, Normandy was attractive for many other reasons including its proximity to the English Channel ports, and the relatively weak German defenses in the region, especially in mid-1943 when Allied planning started in earnest. A two-step solution was found to the problem of port facilities. In the short term, the Allies would rely on the creation of a pair of artificial harbors that would be located at the landing beaches. The next objective would be to seize suitable port facilities. This was a task assigned to the US Army: first, the seizure of Cherbourg and then the Breton ports. Utah Beach was selected with this objective in mind. It was the westernmost of the five

---

1 Campaign 100: *D-Day 1944 (1) Omaha Beach*

This propaganda photo of the Atlantic Wall was released by Germany in December 1943. The Cotentin peninsula, especially around Cherbourg, was one of the few portions of the Normandy coast with a substantial number of heavy coastal defense guns like these. (USAOM)

D-Day landing beaches, at the base of the Cotentin peninsula, offering the best access toward Cherbourg.

German defense of the Cotentin peninsula was based on the mistaken assessment that the main Allied effort would be against the Pas de Calais. As a result, German defensive efforts in 1943 concentrated on creating the "Atlantic Wall" along this stretch of coastline. The Allied landings in Italy in 1943–44, particularly the Anzio landing in January 1944, convinced senior German commanders that the Allies would land in more than one location, using smaller landings to draw off German reserves and weaken the main defenses. As a result, the German strategy was to deploy second-rate units behind mediocre beach defenses on other areas of the French coast such as Normandy and Brittany as an economy-of-force approach. These forces would prevent an uncontested Allied landing and would be reinforced in early 1944 as resources permitted.

CHRONOLOGY

1943

July First draft of Overlord plan completed
3 November Führer Directive 51 directs priority to reinforcing Western Front
6 November Rommel appointed to lead Army Group for Special Employment

1944

1 February Operation Neptune plan adds Utah Beach to the Overlord operation
28 May Landing zone for 82nd Airborne Div. shifted from St Sauveur to Merderet River
3 June OSS teams drop into Normandy to set up beacons for pathfinders
4 June Luftwaffe meteorologist forecasts rough seas and gale-force winds through mid-June
5 June Eisenhower decides that break in weather will permit execution of Neptune on 6 June 1944

D-Day, Tuesday, 6 June, 1944

00.15 Pathfinders begin landing in Normandy to set up beacons for air drops
01.30 Albany mission begins and 101st Airborne paratroopers start landing in Normandy
02.30 Boston mission begins and 82nd Airborne paratroopers start landing in Normandy
02.30 Task Force U arrives off Utah Beach, anchors in transport area
03.10 Gen Marcks begins to move Kampfgruppe Meyer to counter paratroop drops
04.00 Chicago mission begins and 101st Airborne gliders start landing
04.07 Detroit mission begins and 82nd Airborne gliders start landing
04.30 Cavalry detachment lands on St Marcouf island off Utah Beach, finds it deserted
05.05 German coastal batteries begin engaging Allied warships
05.50 Preliminary naval bombardment of Utah Beach begins
06.05 Bomber attacks on Utah Beach begin
06.30 Assault waves begin landing on Utah Beach
09.00 Combat Team 8 (CT8) begins moving off Utah Beach via Exit 2
21.00 Elmira mission delivers glider reinforcements to LZ W; Keokuk to LZ E

POST-D-DAY

7 June Galveston mission delivers gliders to LZ W at 07.00; Hackensack at 09.00
7 June German counterattack on Ste Mère-Église repulsed with tank support
8 June Rommel receives set of captured VII Corps orders, decides to reinforce Cotentin peninsula
9 June La Fière causeway finally captured by 82nd Airborne Division
10 June 101st Airborne seizes causeway leading to Carentan
10 June 90th Division begins attempt to cut off Cotentin peninsula
11 June Fallshirmjäger Regiment 6 (FJR 6) retreats from Carentan
12 June 101st Airborne occupies Carentan in effort to link up with V Corps at Omaha Beach
13 June Counterattack on Carentan by 17th SS-Panzergrenadier Division fails with heavy losses
15 June Failure of 90th Division leads to substitution of 9th Division and 82nd Airborne Div. in westward attack
16 June Hitler meets Rommel and Rundstedt in France, insists on last-ditch defense of Cherbourg
17 June 60th Infantry, 9th Division reaches the sea at Barneville, cutting off Cotentin peninsula
19 June Final drive on Cherbourg begins as a three-division assault
21 June VII Corps reaches outer ring of defenses of Fortress Cherbourg
25 June US infantry begin entering outskirts of Cherbourg
26 June Senior Wehrmacht commanders in Cherbourg forced to surrender
28 June Final outlying German positions in Cherbourg harbor surrender
30 June Last pocket on Cap de la Hague surrender to 9th Division
1 July 9th Division reports that all organized German resistance on Cotentin peninsula has ended

OPPOSING COMMANDERS

GERMAN COMMANDERS

The Wehrmacht had developed a hard-won reputation for tactical excellence during World War II, due in large measure to a style of war epitomized by "*aufsträgtaktik*": senior commanders briefed their subordinate commanders on the goals of the mission, and then permitted them to carry out the assignment as they saw fit, allowing them considerable tactical flexibility. This flexibility was eroded as the conflict dragged on, particularly in the final year of the war. By 1944, the Wehrmacht's capabilities in the field were degraded by an increasingly Byzantine command structure. At the strategic level, Hitler had gradually usurped more and more command authority due to his growing distrust of the professional army officers. He made all major strategic decisions, but interfered at the tactical level as well. Given the sheer complexity of modern industrial war, management of combat operations was beyond the capabilities of a single great commander as might have been possible in centuries before. Hitler's interference was inevitably erratic and episodic. He would allow the usual chains of command to exercise control over most operations, but would become involved in some operations at his whim. Hitler's leadership style was more feudal than modern, encouraging the dispersion of power away from professional organizations like the general staff and into the hands of enthusiastic amateurs like himself, cronies such as the Luftwaffe head Hermann Göring and the SS chief, Heinrich Himmler.

Field command was in the hands of the professionals, but with inefficient constraints on their freedom of action. **Generalfeldmarschal Gerd von Rundstedt** was the nominal supreme commander of western forces (OB West). In reality the Luftwaffe and Navy units in the West were outside his jurisdiction, and some occupation units were under the control of regional governors. Rundstedt's control was further confused by Hitler's decision in the autumn of 1943 to dispatch one of his favorites, **Generalfeldmarschal Erwin Rommel**, to command the amorphous "invasion front". Rommel and Rundstedt attempted to cooperate under difficult circumstances. Rommel took it upon himself to reinvigorate the construction of beach defenses along the Channel coast. This had the greatest impact in Normandy, which had previously been neglected. Rommel was less certain than many senior commanders about the inevitability of landings on the Pas de Calais, and felt that even if the main attack did fall there, there still might be significant secondary operations on other coasts. At his instigation, coastal defenses in Normandy were significantly strengthened during the winter and spring of 1943–44. Rommel's role eventually became the leadership of Army Group B, which clarified his command relationship with Rundstedt. However, this could

Commander of Army Group B was Field Marshal Erwin Rommel. It was Rommel's initiative in the autumn of 1943 that set in motion the fortification of the Normandy beaches. (MHI)

A veteran Panzer commander from the Russian front, GenIt Karl von Schlieben commanded the 709th Infantry Division, which defended the Normandy coast from Utah Beach to Cherbourg. In late June, he was placed in charge of Fortress Cherbourg by Hitler. (NARA)

The hapless 91st Luftlande Division had three commanders within a few days after Gen Wilhelm Falley was killed by paratroopers on D-Day. He was finally succeeded by Generalmajor Eugen König seen here. (NARA)

not solve the divergent tactical approaches sought by the two senior commanders. Rommel and Rundstedt had serious disagreements over the way that reserve Panzer formations should be deployed, an argument that proved even more complicated due to Hitler's personal interest and involvement in the issue. This controversy was not settled prior to the invasion, and indeed continued to rage through most of June 1944 even after the Allied landings.

Defense of the Cotentin peninsula was the responsibility of the 7th Army, responsible for all German army units along the Normandy coast and Brittany and commanded by **Generaloberst Friedrich Dollman**. Dollman was a corps commander in Poland in 1939, assigned command of the 7th Army in the battle of France in 1940, and remained in command during the years of occupation. Some Eastern Front veterans serving in France felt that the years of occupation duty had softened him and his staff. Dollman died of a heart attack on 28 June 1944, less than a month after D-Day.

The Normandy sector, including the Cotentin peninsula, was the responsibility of the 84th Infantry Corps commanded by **General der Infanterie Erich Marcks**. He was a highly regarded commander and served as a staff officer in Poland in 1939 and France in 1940. He was involved in the planning for Operation Barbarossa, and commanded the 101st Jäger Division at the time of the invasion of the Soviet Union in 1941. After he lost a leg in combat in Russia, he was reassigned to the command of the 337th Infantry Division following his recuperation. His skills as a divisional commander led to his elevation to army corps command, first the 66th Corps in September 1942, then the 87th Corps. The Nazis considered him politically suspect as he had been an aide to General von Schleicher, murdered by the SS in 1934, and he was passed over by Hitler for army command. Instead, he was assigned to the 84th Corps in France on 1 August 1943 as part of the process to refresh the command structure in France with Eastern Front veterans. The 84th Corps headquarters was located at St Lô. Marcks was killed in Normandy during an air attack on 12 June 1944.

Utah Beach fell within the defense zone of the 709th Infantry Division, commanded by **Generalleutnant Karl Wilhelm von Schlieben**. He was appointed to command the division in December 1943 as part of the process to refresh occupation forces in France with hardened veterans from the Eastern Front. He was not the most likely officer to be assigned to a static division, having spent most of the war in the Panzer forces. He had commanded a Panzergrenadier regiment, a rifle brigade, and then 18th Panzer Division in two and a half years of fighting in Russia. The western side of the Cotentin peninsula was defended by another static division, the 243rd Infantry Division, commanded by **Generalleutnant Heinz Hellmich**. The division had been raised in July 1943, and Hellmich was its second commander, assigned on 10 January 1944. Hellmich was killed in action on 17 June 1944. A third division, the newly formed 91st Luftlande Division, was sent to the Cotentin peninsula in May 1944 and had been commanded by **Generalleutnant Wilhelm Falley** since 25 April 1944.

Of the three divisional commanders in this sector, two were in Rennes on D-Day participating in a *Kriegsspiel* (wargame) along with many of their staff. Schlieben did not arrive back at his command post in Valognes until

noon, and Falley was killed by US paratroops near Picauville while returning to his headquarters around dawn. Command of the 91st Luftlande Division was temporarily taken over by **Generalmajor Bernhard Klosterkemper** later on D-Day, awaiting the arrival of a new commander, **Generalmajor Eugen König**, who was assigned the post on 7 June. He arrived at the command post on the afternoon of 10 June.

AMERICAN COMMANDERS

The First US Army was responsible for the conduct of the D-Day landings and was commanded by **Lieutenant General Omar Bradley**. The assault force for Operation Neptune consisted of the V Corps at Omaha Beach and the VII Corps at Utah Beach. VII Corps was commanded by **Major General J. Lawton Collins**, better known by his nickname, "Lightning Joe". Collins graduated from West Point in April 1917, but did not arrive in Europe until after the Armistice. He received a divisional command in May 1942, taking over the 25th Division in the Pacific. Formed from cadres of the peacetime Hawaiian Division, this unit had a poor reputation. Collins whipped it into shape for its first assignment, relieving the 1st Marine Division on Guadalcanal in early 1943. The codename for the division headquarters on Guadalcanal was "Lightning", from which Collins picked up his nickname. He had been brought back from the Pacific theater to provide combat experience. Bradley described him as "independent, heady, capable, and full of vinegar" and he would prove to be one of the most aggressive and talented US field commanders in Europe. He later served as the army chief of staff during the Korean War.

With few exceptions, Collins was blessed with excellent commanders. Not surprisingly, the two airborne division commanders stood out. The 82nd Airborne Division had been commanded by **Major General Matthew Ridgway** since June 1942 when it had first converted from a regular infantry division into a paratroop division. Ridgway had led the unit during

One of the most highly regarded infantry commanders in Normandy was MajGen Manton Eddy, commander of the 9th Infantry Division, seen here talking over a field telephone during the fighting in Cherbourg at the end of June 1944. (MHI)

The first major American victory in France was the capture of Cherbourg, and "Lightning Joe" Collins is seen here on a hill overlooking the port talking to Capt Kirkpatrick from the 79th Division. (MHI)

its first major combat jump over Sicily in 1943, and after the Normandy operation would be pushed upstairs to lead the XVIII Airborne Corps in time for Operation Market Garden in September 1944. He would go on to a distinguished career after the war as supreme NATO commander and army chief of staff. The 101st Airborne Division was led by **Major General Maxwell Taylor**, who had served as the artillery commander of the 82nd Airborne Division during the Sicily campaign. Taylor became best known for a cloak-and-dagger affair in 1943 when he was smuggled into Rome to confer with Italian officers about a plan to land the 82nd Airborne Division to capture the city. Taylor quickly appreciated that the hare-brained scheme would lead to the destruction of the division, and he was able to avert it in the nick of time. He also enjoyed a distinguished post-war career, and was the Army chief of staff in the mid-1950s after Collins.

The infantry division leading the assault on Utah Beach was the 4th Infantry Division, commanded by **Major General Raymond "Tubby" Barton** since July 1942. Barton led the division through the autumn campaign, culminating in the ferocious Hürtgen Forest campaign that gutted the division. He was relieved for medical reasons by George Patton in December 1944. His assistant divisional commander was **Brigadier General Theodore Roosevelt Jr.**, son of president Teddy Roosevelt, and a distinguished soldier in his own right. Roosevelt had been assistant commander of the 1st Infantry Division in North Africa and Sicily, and when the divisional commander was relieved in 1943 due to personality conflicts with Bradley, Roosevelt was given the boot as well. He was reassigned to the 4th Division, where he proved to be a popular and effective leader. He died in Normandy from a heart attack, but his inspirational leadership at Utah Beach led to his posthumous decoration with the Medal of Honor.

Following the initial phase of the Utah Beach operation, the 82nd and 101st Airborne Divisions were withdrawn to Britain for refitting. Three other infantry divisions would play a central role in the fighting on the Cotentin peninsula. The 9th Infantry Division, headed by **Major General Manton Eddy**, was a veteran of the North Africa and Sicily fighting and widely regarded as one of the army's best divisions. Eddy was a particularly capable officer and in August was given command of the XII Corps in Patton's Third Army. The 79th Division was commanded by **Major General Ira Wyche**, West Point class of 1911. Wyche had served in the field artillery until assigned to command the 79th Division in May 1942, leading it in its combat debut in 1944. Of all the divisions in Collins' VII Corps, the only one to suffer from serious leadership problems was the 90th Division, led by **Major General Jay MacKelvie**. An artilleryman by training, MacKelvie had little feel for infantry operations and was relieved by Collins on 12 June after five days of combat along with two of his regimental commanders.

OPPOSING ARMIES

GERMAN FORCES

By the summer of 1944, the Wehrmacht had been bled white by three years of brutal conflict in Russia. The enormous personnel demands of the Eastern Front led to the cannibalization of units in France. Hitler "wanted to be stronger than mere facts" and so the Wehrmacht order of battle became increasingly fanciful in the last year of the war, with impressive paper strength but increasingly emaciated forces.

In response to Rundstedt's strong criticism of the state of the forces in France in October 1943, Hitler issued Führer Directive 51 to reinvigorate the Wehrmacht in the West. Rundstedt's command increased from 46 to 58 divisions, partly from the transfer of burned-out divisions from the Eastern Front to France for rebuilding, and partly from newly formed divisions. The units on the Cotentin peninsula were second-rate formations. In 1942 Rundstedt had initiated the formation of static divisions. These were under strength compared to normal infantry divisions, lacked the usual reconnaissance battalion, and had only three battalions of artillery. In addition, their personnel were mostly from older age groups. Through much of the autumn of 1943, the better troops were siphoned off to satisfy the insatiable requirements for more replacements on the Eastern Front. In their place came a steady stream of Ost battalions manned by "volunteers" from Red Army prisoners. Colonel Von der Heydte of the 6th Fallschirmjäger Regiment recalled that: "The troops for a defense against an Allied landing were not comparable to those committed in Russia. Their morale was low; the majority of the enlisted men and noncommissioned officers lacked combat experience; and the

A severe shortage of German conscripts prompted the Wehrmacht to employ former Soviet prisoners-of-war in infantry units. This soldier, from one of the Soviet Union's Central Asian republics, wears the swastika-less eagle insignia peculiar to these troops above his right breast pocket. (NARA)

Many German units on the Cotentin peninsula were over-extended, second-rate units. The lack of motor transport led to expedients such as the use of bicycles in some units such as the 243rd Infantry Division. This is a bicycle-borne *Panzerschreck* anti-tank rocket unit. Note that the lead bicycle carries spare rockets in a seat over the rear wheel. (MHI)

officers were in the main those who, because of lack of qualification or on account of wounds or illness were no longer fit for service on the Eastern Front." The weapons were "from all over the world and seem to have been accumulated from all periods of the twentieth century." For example, during the fighting along a 1¼ mile (2km) stretch of the Carentan front, von der Heydte's unit was equipped with four calibers of mortars from 78mm to 82mm, of German, French, Italian, and Soviet design. General Marcks summed up his assessment during the Cherbourg maneuvers in 1944: "Emplacements without guns, ammunition depots without ammunition, minefields without mines, and a large number of men in uniform with hardly a soldier among them."

The occupation divisions were bedeviled by the petty mindset of an army assigned to years of peaceful occupation duty. General Schlieben recalled that "For someone who had served only in the east, the flood of orders, directives, and regulations which continually showered the troops was a novelty for me. This paper flood impressed me more than the tide along the Atlantic coast. Higher headquarters concerned themselves with trivial affairs of subordinate commanders. For example, it became a problem whether a machine-gun was to be placed 20 meters more to the right or the left ... A senior commander wanted to have an old ramshackle hut demolished to create a better field of fire so a written application had to be filed with the appropriate area HQ, accompanied by a sketch." This practice began to change in February–March 1944 after Rommel's arrival. Rommel was insistent that beach defenses be strengthened. There were not enough workers from the paramilitary Organization Todt to carry out this work, since they were involved in the construction of a series of massive concrete bases for the secret V-1 and V-2 missiles. Instead, the construction work was carried out by the infantry in these sectors, at the expense of their combat training.

The 709th Infantry Division deployed *Goliath* remote control demolition vehicles from special underground hiding places as seen here. They were popularly called "doodlebugs" or "beetles" by the US troops who found many on the beach or in the countryside beyond. (NARA)

The 709th Infantry Division defending Utah Beach provides a clear example of the problems. The division had been formed in May 1941 as an occupation division and in November 1942 it was converted into a static division. One of its battalions was sent to Russia in October 1943, and in June 1944 three of its 11 infantry battalions were manned by former Red Army prisoners of war. Two of these were attached Ost battalions formed from various Red Army prisoners while another was recruited from Georgian prisoners. The division was further weakened by the incorporation of a high percentage of troops recruited from *Volkliste III*, mostly Poles from border areas incorporated into Germany after 1939. The divisional commander later noted that their reliability in combat was doubtful, and he did not expect that the eastern battalions would "fight hard in cases of emergency." German troops in the division were over age with an average

The workhorse of the German infantry divisions was the StuG III Ausf. G assault gun which combined the excellent 75mm anti-tank gun on the old PzKpfw III chassis. This one was knocked out in the fighting near Ste Mère-Église with the 82nd Airborne Division. (NARA)

German units in France exploited the large inventory of captured French armored vehicles to flesh out their meager armored reserves. The small Renault R-35 infantry tank was fitted with a Czech 47mm anti-tank gun, resulting in a lightly armed and thinly armored tank destroyer. On the Cotentin peninsula, these vehicles served with Panzer Abteilung 101, a training unit attached to the 709th Infantry Division. (NARA)

German Panzer forces on the Cotentin penisula were mostly composed of training units equipped with obsolete, captured French tanks. The Hotchkiss H-39 of Pz.Abt. 100 would figure prominently in the fighting against the paratroopers around Utah Beach. (NARA)

of 36 years. In spite of the mediocre quality of the troops, the division was relatively large for a static division with 12,320 men, and it had 11 infantry battalions instead of the nine found in the new pattern 1944 infantry divisions. Of these troops, 333 were Georgian volunteers and 1,784 were former Red Army POWs. The divisional artillery had three battalions; one with mixed French/Czech equipment, the second with French guns, and the third with Soviet guns. For anti-tank defense, it had 12 towed 75mm anti-tank guns and 9 self-propelled 75mm tank destroyers. Tank support was provided by Panzer Abteilung 101, a training unit weakly equipped with ten Panzerjäger 35R, an improvised combination of Czech 47mm anti-tank guns on obsolete French Renault R-35 chassis. The division originally was spread along the entire Cotentin coastline, a distance of some 150 miles (240km). With the arrival of the 243rd Infantry Division in May, its

frontage was reduced. It still stretched from Utah Beach all the way to the northern coast around Cherbourg, a distance of about 60 miles (100km). As a result, its defenses were simply a thin crust along the shore with very little depth. Rommel hoped to compensate for the paucity of men with concrete defenses, but the construction along the Cotentin coast received less priority than in other sectors.

The 243rd Infantry Division was formed in July 1943 as a static division and reorganized in January 1944. Two of its infantry battalions were converted from static units to bicycle infantry, though in the process, the division lost an infantry battalion. The division was originally in reserve, but in late May was shifted to

A large group of GIs from the 4th Infantry Division are seen on the deck of an assault transport on the way to Utah Beach in June 1944. (NARA)

defend the western coast, taking over from the over-extended 709th Infantry Division. On D-Day it included about 11,530 troops, somewhat under strength. Its artillery was mostly captured Soviet types, but it had a self-propelled tank destroyer battalion with 14 75mm Marder III and ten StuG III assault guns. The division was reinforced by Panzer Abteilung 206, equipped with a hodgepodge of old French tanks including 20 Hotchkiss H-39, 10 Somua S-35, 2 Renault R-35 and 6 Char B1 *bis*. This was deployed on the Cap de la Hague on the northwestern tip of the Cotentin peninsula.

The 91st Luftlande Division was formed in January 1944 to take part in Operation *Tanne* (pine tree), an aborted airborne operation in Scandanavia planned for March 1944. When this mission fell through, the partially formed division was transferred to Normandy, arriving in May

Tank support for Combat Team 8 came from the 70th Tank Battalion. Several M4 and M4A1 medium tanks of Company C are seen here fitted with deep wading trunks for the Utah Beach landing while in the foreground, one of the unit's T2 tank recovery vehicles backs on board the landing craft before setting off from Kingswear, Devon, England. (NARA)

Additional armored support for Utah Beach came from the 899th Tank Destroyer Battalion, which later played a role in the efforts to overcome the German coastal fortifications at Crisbecq and Azeville. Here a number of M10 3in. Gun Motor Carriages with deep wading trunks are loaded aboard LSTs in England for the D-Day operation. (NARA)

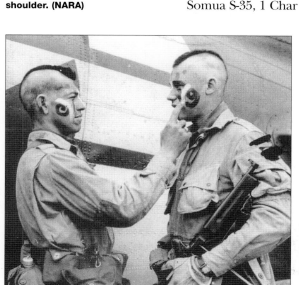

Some paratroopers of the 506th PIR, 101st Airborne Division, decided to get Mohican haircuts and daub their faces with their idea of Indian warpaint. This is demolition specialist Clarence Ware applying the finishing touches to Pvt Charles Plaudo. The censor has obscured the "screaming eagle" divisional patch on his shoulder. (NARA)

1944 to reinforce the two static divisions. At the time of the invasion, it was under strength with only two infantry regiments and a single fusilier battalion, and numbered about 7,500 men. However, 6th Fallschirmjäger Regiment (FJR 6) from the 2nd Fallschirmjäger Division was attached to the division during the Normandy fighting. Colonel Von der Heydte of FJR 6 considered that the combat efficiency of the division was poor, especially compared to his elite Luftwaffe troops. The division artillery was based around the 105mm Gebirgs-haubitze 40 mountain gun, which did not share the same type of ammunition as the normal 105mm divisional gun. Once the division had expended its one basic load of ammunition, its guns were useless. During the course of the fighting, its artillery regiment was re-armed with a mixture of captured artillery types including Czech and Soviet types. Panzer Abteilung 100, headquartered at Château de Francquetot, provided armored support. It had a motley collection of captured French tanks including 17 Renault R-35, 8 Hotchkiss H-39, one Somua S-35, 1 Char B1 *bis*, and 1 PzKpfw III.

There were a number of smaller formations in the area as well. Sturm-Abteilung AOK 7 was an assault infantry battalion attached to the Seventh Army headquarters. On D-Day, it was redeployed from Cherbourg to the 701st Infantry Division during its actions near the Vire River.

Even if the German units on the Cotentin peninsula were not the best in the Wehrmacht, they were still a credible fighting force. Training and tactics were based on hard-won battle experience, and there were Eastern Front veterans in many of the divisions. During the fighting, General Barton visited one of his battalions that had been stalled by the German defenses and assured the officers that the German troops facing them were second-rate. A young lieutenant replied: "General, I think you'd better put the Germans on the distribution list. They don't seem to realize that!"

Besides the infantry formations, there were a significant number of coastal gun batteries located around the Cotentin peninsula. The army controlled two coastal artillery regiments (*Heeres-küsten-artillerie-abteilung*), HKAA 1262 on the west coast of the peninsula and HKAA 1261 on the east coast. Some of these took part in the later land actions, most notably the Azeville and Crisbecq battery of HKAA 1261 near St Marcouf. The navy's MAA 260 (*Marine-artillerie-abteilung*) was responsible for the seven naval batteries located mainly in the area around Cherbourg while MAA 608 protected the port of Granville on the western side of the peninsula.

Order of battle: German Units, Cotentin Peninsula, June 1944

84th Corps	St Lô	General der Artillerie Erich Marcks
709th Infantry Division	*Chiffremont*	*Generalleutnant Karl von Schlieben*
Grenadier Regiment 729	Le Vast	
Grenadier Regiment 739	Cherbourg	
Grenadier Regiment 919	Quineville	
243rd Infantry Division	*Bricquebec*	*Generalleutnant Heinz Hellmich*
Grenadier Regiment 920	Quett	
Grenadier Regiment 921	Lessay	
Grenadier Regiment 922	Sortosville	
91st Luftlande Division	*Etienville*	*Generalmajor Wilhelm Falley*
Grenadier Regiment 1057	Hauteville	
Grenadier Regiment 1058	Vindefontaine	
Fallschirmjäger Regiment 6	Hotellerie	
Coastal Artillery Units		
Army Coastal Artillery Regiment 1261	Quineville	Oberst Gerhard Triepel
Army Coastal Artillery Regiment 1262	Grosseville	
Naval Artillery Regiment 260	Cherbourg	Korvettenkapitän Karl Weise
Naval Artillery Regiment 608	Granville	Korvettenkapitän Hubbert

US FORCES

The US units taking part in the initial landings contained the two best light infantry divisions in the army, the 82nd and 101st Airborne Divisions. The 82nd Airborne Division had already seen combat in Sicily and Italy, though in June 1944, more than half of its paratroopers were replacements. Normandy was the first combat jump for the 101st Airborne Division, but like the 82nd, it was formed on the basis of volunteer troops and had exceptionally thorough training. In addition, its officer ranks were stiffened by transferring veterans from the 82nd Airborne Division. Both were elite units in the true sense of the word.

The 4th Infantry Division had been reactivated in 1940 and at first was equipped as a motorized infantry division. This concept was eventually dropped, and the division reverted back to a conventional organization in August 1943 prior to being sent to England. While Bradley had insisted on using at least one experienced division in the assault at neighboring Omaha Beach, Utah Beach was viewed as a less demanding mission. Nevertheless, it required the use of a well-trained and ably led division, and

the 4th Division was chosen. The assault would be conducted by Combat Team 8 (CT8) with the division's 8th Infantry Regiment forming its core.

Armored support for CT8 came from the 70th Tank Battalion, the most experienced separate tank battalion in the US Army, which had previously seen combat as a light tank battalion in North Africa and Sicily. For D-Day, two of its companies were equipped with M4A1 Duplex Drive (DD) amphibious tanks. These tanks were modified by the addition of a folding canvas skirt to provide buoyancy, and a pair of propellers for propulsion in the water. In order to deal with beach obstacles, especially the seawall, there were plans to equip the third medium tank company with 7.2in. demolition rockets in a T40 launcher over the turret. The first four rocket launchers were delivered in May and tested against simulated beach obstructions. The rockets were not particularly effective, but the tank crews showed that two or three high explosive rounds from the tank's 75mm gun were adequate to breach seawalls. As a result, Company C was landed without the rocket launchers. The battalion's light tank company was landed later on D-Day and assigned to support the 82nd Airborne Division.

In the build-up immediately after D-Day, three more infantry divisions were gradually injected into the Cotentin fighting. The 90th Division was based around National Guard units raised in the Texas–Oklahoma area, hence its nickname "Tough Ombres". It developed a bad reputation in Normandy due to poor leadership, which in turn led to poor training. It

went through a series of leadership changes and by the fall, the problems had been largely corrected. It fought with distinction with Patton's Third Army in Lorraine in September 1944. In contrast, the 9th Division was widely regarded as one of the army's best infantry divisions, with previous combat experience in North Africa and Sicily. It would play a critical role in the capture of Cherbourg. The 79th Division was activated in 1942 and shipped to Britain in April 1944. It was a fairly typical US infantry division with good training and leadership.

One of the most significant Allied advantages was the availability of continual air support. At this stage of the war, cooperation between ground and air units was still in a formative stage, and did not come to fruition until late July during Operation Cobra. Nevertheless, continual air operations over the Cotentin peninsula by roving fighter-bombers made any concentrated daytime movement by German units impossible. Some measure of air power's impact can be surmised from the significant percentage of senior German commanders killed by air attack while trying to move between their units.

Order of Battle: US Army, Cotentin Peninsula, June 1944

VII Corps	MajGen J. Lawton Collins
4th Division	*MajGen Raymond Barton*
8th Infantry	Col James Van Fleet
12th Infantry	Col Russell Reeder
22nd Infantry	LtCol James Luckett
9th Division	*MajGen Manton Eddy*
39th Infantry	Col Harry Flint
47th Infantry	Col George Smythe
60th Infantry	Col Frederick de Rohan
79th Division	*MajGen Ira Wyche*
313th Infantry	Col Sterling Wood
314th Infantry	Col Warren Robinson
315th Infantry	Col Poter Wiggins
82nd Airborne Division	*MajGen Matthew Ridgway*
505th Parachute Infantry	Col William Ekman
507th Parachute Infantry	Col George Millett Jr.
508th Parachute Infantry	Col Roy Lindquist
325th Glider Infantry	Col Harry Lewis
90th Division	*BrigGen Jay MacKelvie*
357th Infantry	Col Philip Ginder
358th Infantry	Col James Thompson
359th Infantry	Col Clarke Fales
101st Airborne Division	*MajGen Maxwell Taylor*
501st Parachute Infantry	Col Howard Johnson
502nd Parachute Infantry	Col George Moseley Jr.
506th Parachute Infantry	Col Robert Sink
327th Glider Infantry	Col George Wear
4th Cavalry Group	*Col Joseph Tully*
4th Cavalry Squadron	LtCol E.C. Dunn
24th Cavalry Squadron	LtCol F.H. Gaston Jr.
6th Armored Group	*Col Francis Fainter*
70th Tank Battalion	LtCol John Welbron
746th Tank Battalion	LtCol C.G. Hupfer

OPPOSING PLANS

US PLANS

The original Operation Overlord plans did not envision any Allied landings to the west of the Vire River at the base of the Cotentin peninsula. In January 1944 when General Montgomery was first briefed, he insisted that the frontage of the assault be widened. Montgomery was not entirely convinced of the viability of the artificial harbors and wanted a landing west of the Vire to facilitate an early capture of Cherbourg. The preliminary Operation Neptune plan of 1 February 1944 and the First US Army (FUSA) plan of 25 February expanded the US beachheads to two, one in the Grandcamps sectors (Omaha), and one further east near Les Dunes de Varreville (Utah).

Although many beaches on the eastern Cotentin coast were suitable for landing, the areas behind the beach were a problem since many had been flooded by the Germans. Access between the beach and inland areas was over a small number of narrow causeways that could be defended easily by small German detachments. The second problem was the terrain of the peninsula itself. The Douve River runs through the center of the peninsula, and the low-lying areas of the peninsula were naturally marshy. The Germans exploited this to reduce the number of possible airborne landings by using locks to flood many lowland fields. The planners wanted a beach with at least four causeways to permit the transit of a single division off the beach on D-Day, compared to two on neighboring Omaha Beach. The coast immediately west of Omaha Beach was the obvious solution.

The Cotentin coast was dotted with coastal artillery batteries, including the St Marcouf battery of 3/1261 HKAA in Crisbecq. This ferro-concrete Bauform 683 casemate was armed with a Czech Skoda 210mm gun of the type ordered by Sweden and Turkey but taken over by Germany in 1938. The prolonged defense of the position earned its commander, Oberleutnant zur See Ohmsen, the Knight's Cross after he escaped to Cherbourg on 14 June. (NARA)

One of the most effective types of bunker on the Normandy coast was the Bauform 667 casemate, which were positioned parallel to the shore to permit enfilade fire along the beach. This Bauform 667 casemate of the W5 strongpoint at Utah Beach was armed with a 50mm anti-tank gun, and it was knocked out by tank gun fire directed against the embrasure from close range. (NARA)

To make certain that the causeways remained open, an airborne division would be landed behind the beach before H-Hour on D-Day. Many planners were reluctant to place too much faith on paratroop operations, especially in light of the fiasco on Sicily in 1943. On that occasion the aircraft transporting the 82nd Airborne Division were brought under fire by the naval forces, and the paratroopers subsequently landed in widely scattered and ineffective groups. However, Eisenhower believed that the Sicily operation had merely shown that the airborne force had to land in a more concentrated fashion, and he agreed with General Ridgway to expand the existing US airborne divisions. The initial plan in February envisioned using the 101st Airborne Division immediately behind Utah Beach to secure the causeways. Bradley's FUSA planners wanted the 82nd Airborne dropped further west to permit a rapid cutoff of the Cotentin peninsula, preventing the Germans from reinforcing Cherbourg.

These plans were viewed as extremely risky but Eisenhower decided that they were essential to the operation and that the risks would have to be accepted. The plans continued to evolve well into May, only days before D-Day. Allied intelligence learned of the move of the German 91st Luftlande Division into the central Cotentin peninsula in mid-May. This made the planned landing of the 82nd Airborne Division around St Sauveur-le-Vicomte too risky. Instead, its drop zone was shifted to the Merderet River area, and the 101st Airborne drop zone was shifted slightly south so that both divisions would control an easily defensible area between the beaches and the Douve and Merderet rivers.

GERMAN PLANS

German defensive plans were in a state of flux due to serious disagreements between Rundstedt and Rommel over the deployment and control of the Panzer reserve. To some extent this debate was irrelevant to the Cotentin peninsula, since no senior German commander was particularly concerned that this area would be the focus of an Allied invasion. Until May 1944, the defense of the entire 155 miles (250km) of coastline on the Cotentin peninsula was the responsibility of a single

There was considerable controversy among senior Allied commanders about how to use gliders to reinforce the paratroopers. Here a C-47 of the 90th Troop Carrier Squadron (TCS), 438th TCG (Troop Carrier Group) lifts off from Greenham Common with a Horsa glider in tow on 6 June 1944. (NARA)

Like a medieval knight, a fully loaded paratrooper sometimes needed help simply to move due to the enormous weight of gear and equipment he carried. This is T/4 Joseph Gorenc of the 506th PIR climbing aboard a C-47 on the evening of 5 June 1944. (NARA)

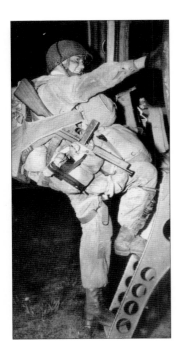

second-rate division. The western coast was lightly guarded since the navy had argued that the heavy seas off the west coast as well as the heavily defended Channel Islands made amphibious landings unlikely. In mid-May, the navy staff had a change of heart, and began to suggest that the Allies might land on both the east and west coasts, with simultaneous attacks on either side of Cherbourg. Shortly afterwards, Rommel visited the area, and later had a conference with Dollman and Marcks about the state of defenses in this sector. Von Schlieben argued that the port facilities in Cherbourg should be sabotaged immediately to make the port an unattractive target, and to permit units to withdraw to the base of the Cotentin peninsula rather than becoming trapped. The navy would not even consider such a plan and the proposal was ignored. Instead, the defense of the Cotentin peninsula was substantially increased. The 243rd Infantry Division was shifted from its location further south in reserve, and placed along the west coast. The partially formed 91st Luftlande Division was placed at the base of the peninsula to back up the two static divisions.

Defense of the Cotentin coast did not have as high a priority as other sectors further east, which were judged to be more likely objectives for an Allied amphibious assault. The forces along the coast were spread very thin, locally concentrated in strongpoints "like a string of pearls." Defenses were not particularly heavy along Utah Beach, since it was presumed that such a beach would be an unattractive objective given the tidal marshes behind it. Two battalions of GR.919 held a total of 25 strongpoints from Le Grand Vey in the south to the Aumeville beach in the north, a distance of about 15 miles (25km). The strongpoints were categorized into two types, *wiederstandnest* (Wn = reinforced position) and *stutzpunkt* (StP = support position). These strongpoints typically consisted of a platoon of 40 troops with several small bunkers, a few machine-gun pits or concrete reinforced "Tobruks", and a few anti-tank guns or obsolete field guns. To make up for the shortage of troops, the formations along the coast had more firepower than a normal infantry unit, even though the weapons were a motley selection of obsolete or captured types.

Paratroopers of the 101st Airborne have their chutes and equipment checked by Lt Bobuck prior to boarding their C-47 for the flight to Normandy. The C-47 in the background has had the black and white D-Day invasion stripes hastily painted on. (NARA)

The strongpoint that figured most directly in the subsequent fighting was WN5. It was manned by a platoon from 3./GR.919 and was commanded by Leutnant Arthur Jahnke, a young veteran of the Eastern Front and holder of the Knight's Cross. It included a 50mm anti-tank gun in a Bauform 667 casemate, two 50mm anti-tank guns in open concrete pits, one French 47mm anti-tank gun in a concrete pit, a Bauform 67 with a French tank turret and 37mm gun, four mortar and machine-gun Tobruks, and a half-dozen other bunkers and shelters. One of the platoon's more exotic weapons was a group of *Goliath* remote control demolition vehicles, a type of wire-guided tracked vehicle designed to be used like a land torpedo to attack high-value targets such as tanks and landing craft. These were deployed from small caves facing the beach. A second strongpoint, WN4, was located immediately to the west of WN5, covering the main access causeway off the beach.

The regimental commander, Oberstleutnant Gunther Keil, did not agree with Rommel's tactic of placing all of his troops in the forward bunkers. Instead, he placed a minimal number of troops on the coast, and the rest of each platoon as an "alert unit" (*alarmeinheiten*) in the buildings behind the beach. Artillery in this sector included a battery from Sturm-Abteilung AOK 7 west of Foucarville, and a battery of multiple rocket launchers from I./Nebelwerfer Regiment 100 south of Brucheville. There were also three batteries from an army coastal artillery regiment (HKAA.1261) in this sector; the 1./HKAA.1261 in St Martin-de-Varreville with four ex-Soviet 122mm guns, the 2./HKAA.1261 in Azeville with four French Schneider 105mm guns, and the 3./HKAA 1261 in Crisbecq with three massive 210mm Skoda guns.

Unlike neighboring Omaha Beach, the Utah Beach sector was relatively flat, not affording the excellent fields of fire to be found further east on the coast. The beach obstacles in front of WN5 were far less extensive than those at neighboring Omaha Beach, and the obstacles largely petered out in the area in front of Grande Dune where the landings actually occurred. Although GR.919 had attempted to reinforce these defenses, the tidal conditions simply washed many of the obstacles ashore. The main reserve in this sector was the Georgian Battalion 795 Ost, which was located further west near Criqueville, and GR.1058 from the 91st Luftlande Division located in the central peninsula in the landing zone of the 82nd Airborne Division.

The Kriegsmarine lacked sufficient forces to seriously entertain the idea of repelling the Allied invasion at sea. Marinegruppe West, under Vizeadmiral Theodor Krancke, was divided into sectors with Konteradmiral Rieve's Channel Coast responsible for the Normandy coast through to the Dutch border. The port nearest to Utah Beach was Cherbourg, which contained two torpedo flotillas, totaling 16 S-boats. Krancke had attempted to inhibit the invasion activities by a program of minelaying off the Normandy coast to coincide with Rommel's fortification efforts. Unbeknownst to him, the Allies were aware of the location of nearly all of these minefields due to the breaking of the Enigma codes. In addition, Enigma allowed the Royal Navy to vigorously disrupt minelaying in the weeks before D-Day. Attempts to mine the Seine bay on 24 May were met by a force of British torpedo boats and Coastal Command aircraft that put an end to any further attempts. The lack of bombproof U-boat shelters along the Channel inhibited Krancke from deploying submarines in the invasion area.

The Luftwaffe played virtually no role in the fighting in the Cotentin sector during June. Allied air superiority was so great, and the Luftwaffe so weak that there was little hope for conducting Luftwaffe operations so far west from the air bases near Paris.

On 4 June 1944, Major Lettau, the chief Luftwaffe meteorologist in Paris released a forecast indicating that the Allies were unlikely to launch an invasion over the next fortnight due to rough seas and gale-force winds that were unlikely to weaken until mid-June. This forecast convinced OB West that it would be an appropriate opportunity to conduct a major command wargame in Rennes to study possible counter-strokes against Allied airborne attacks in Normandy. As a result, about half the divisional commanders and a quarter of the regimental commanders were on their way to a wargame in Rennes. Indeed, the weather forecast was so bad that many units were using the opportunity to give their men rest from the strenuous construction program along the coast. Rommel used the spell of bad weather to visit Germany, hoping to convince the Führer to release more Panzers to his control for a forward defense of the coast.

D-DAY

The first troops to land in France in preparation for Operation Neptune were OSS teams (Office of Strategic Service), usually consisting of two US soldiers trained in the operation of signal devices, teamed with three British commandos for site security. A half-dozen of these teams were flown into France around 01.30hrs on 3 June to mark airborne drop zones for later pathfinder teams who would bring in more extensive marking equipment.

The troops of the two airborne divisions began final preparations for the Normandy airdrops on 5 June at 15 separate airfields in southern England. The air delivery of the two divisions was assigned to the IX Troop Carrier command. Operation Albany, the delivery of the 101st Airborne Division, was assigned to the 50th Troop Carrier Wing and Operation Boston, the delivery of the 82nd Airborne Division, was assigned to the 52nd Wing. The initial wave used 821 troop-laden C-47 and C-54 transports. Each aircraft carried a "stick" of paratroopers, usually 18–20 per aircraft in most aircraft, but 9–10 in parachute artillery units due to the amount of other equipment carried.

To conduct a nighttime drop, the transport pilots were dependent on visual and radar signals to locate the drop zone. Pathfinders were parachuted into the drop zones ahead of the main wave to set up both types of signals – a set of seven color-coded Aldis lamps in the shape of a "T" and an AN/PPN-1 "Eureka" radar beacon. The Eureka set was a useful aid for the approach to the drop zone, but became less effective about two miles out, requiring the use of the Aldis signal lamps for the final approach. Nineteen aircraft carrying the pathfinders departed before midnight and they began landing in France around 00.15hrs on 6 June 1944. The following waves of C-47 transports were fitted with a "Rebecca" system to pick up the signal emitted from the Eureka ground beacon, and some were also fitted with "Gee" navigation aids.

On approaching the drop zones, the pathfinder aircraft encountered an unexpected bank of cloud that created navigational problems. In the 101st Airborne sector, only the teams allotted to Drop Zone C parachuted close to the target. Likewise in the 82nd Airborne Division sector, only one batch of pathfinders was accurately dropped into Drop Zone O. In the case of the other four drop zones, the pathfinders were dropped so far away from their target that they did not have enough time after their landing to reach their designated drop-zone. As a result, some of the pathfinder teams set up their landing beacons in areas away from the planned drop zones, while other teams were able to set up only the Eureka beacons since the presence of German troops nearby made it impossible to set up the Aldis lamps.

The main wave of C-47 transports began taking off from England around midnight. The two skytrains coalesced over the English Channel, and then followed a route around the Cotentin peninsula, passing between the Channel Islands, and entering enemy air-space over the west Cotentin coast, heading northeastward toward the drop zone, and exiting over Utah Beach. In parallel, a force of RAF Stirling bombers flew a diversionary mission, dropping chaff to simulate an airborne formation and dropping dummy paratroopers and noisemakers into areas away from the actual drop zones. The weather conditions were a full moon and clearing skies. The flight proved uneventful until the coast, and the aircraft flew in tight formation in a "V-of-Vs". On reaching the coast, the problems began. The aircraft encountered the same dense cloud that had frustrated the pathfinders. The pathfinder transports had not radioed back a warning about this due to radio silence. The clouds created immediate dangers due to the proximity of the aircraft in formation, and C-47s began to frantically maneuver to avoid mid-air collisions. Some pilots climbed to 2,000 feet to avoid the clouds, others descended below the cloud bank to 500 feet, while some remained at the prescribed altitude of 700 feet. This cloud bank completely disrupted the formation and ended any hopes for a concentrated paratroop drop.

Anti-aircraft fire began during the final approach into the drop zones near the coast. Although they had been instructed to maintain a steady course, some pilots began jinking their aircraft to avoid steady streams of 20mm cannon fire. It was an inauspicious start for an inherently risky mission.

Table 1: D-Day Airlift Operations, IX Troop Carrier Command

Mission	Albany	Boston	Total
Aircraft sorties	433	378	811
Aborted sorties	2	1	3
Aircraft lost or missing	13	8	21
Aircraft damaged	81	115	196
Aircrew killed or missing	48	17	65
Aircrew wounded	4	11	15
Troops carried	6,928	6,420	13,348
Troops dropped	6,750	6,350	13,100
Howitzers carried	12	2	14
Cargo carried (tons)	211	178	389

ALBANY MISSION

The 101st Airborne Division was the first to land around 01.30hrs on 6 June 1944. Its primary objective was to seize control of the area behind Utah Beach between St Martin-de-Varreville and Pouppeville to facilitate the exit of the 4th Infantry Division from the beach later that morning. Its secondary mission was to protect the southern flank of VII Corps by destroying two bridges on the Carentan highway and a railroad bridge west of it, gaining control of the Barquette lock, and establishing a bridgehead over the Douve River northeast of Carentan.

The 502nd Parachute Infantry Regiment (PIR) and 506th PIR (less one battalion) were assigned to the primary objective. The first wave of the 502nd PIR consisted of the 2/502nd PIR and HQ/502nd PIR. The transport aircraft carrying these units were scattered by cloud cover and flak, landing far from Drop Zone A. Most of the 2/502nd PIR was dropped compactly but inaccurately on the far edge of Drop Zone C, three miles south of intended Drop Zone A. The battalion landed in an area divided up by a maze of dense hedgerows, the Normandy *bocage*, and had a great deal of difficulty assembling and orienting themselves. These units spent most of D-Day regrouping and took no part in the initial fighting.

The 3/502nd PIR landed in very scattered fashion to the east of Ste Mère-Église. The battalion commander, Lieutenant Colonel Robert Cole, gathered about 75 men and began moving on the coastal battery at St Martin-de-Varreville. They found that the guns had been removed and the position deserted due to pre-invasion bombardment, so they moved on to their next objective, the western side of Audouville–la-Hubert causeway (Exit 3), arriving there around 07.30hrs. German troops of the I/GR.919 abandoning strongpoint WN8 began retreating across this causeway around 09.30hrs and were ambushed by the concealed paratroopers, losing 50–75 men. This battalion also attempted to clear Exit 4, and while they found it undefended, the location of the nearby German batteries made this causeway unusable for exiting the beach. Contact was made with the 4th Infantry Division around 13.00hrs, and the battalion spent the rest of the day collecting their scattered and missing men.

Lieutenant Colonel Patrick Cassidy's 1/502nd PIR landed near St Germain-de-Varreville, with 20 of the 36 aircraft within a mile of the beacon. One group led by Cassidy moved toward the stone buildings near Mésières, the garrison for the German coastal battery at St Martin-de-Varreville. Cassidy's group occupied the crossroads outside Mésières and determined that the two northern exits assigned to his battalion were clear. On meeting another group of about 45 men from his unit, he ordered them north to create a defensive perimeter near Foucarville. Cassidy kept about a company of troops near the crossroads to prevent any intervention against the beach from the west, and sent a squad to the eastern side of Mésières to clean out any German troops. A team led by Staff Sergeant Harrison Summers killed or captured about 150 German troops in a series of one-sided encounters. As this action was winding down, the regimental commander, Lieutenant Colonel John Michaels arrived with 200 men. This freed up the remainder of Cassidy's men at the crossroads, who then followed the other paratroopers to the Foucarville area. Cassidy's force advanced to

Paratroopers sit on the canvas benches along the fuselage of the C-47 during the trip to Normandy with a captain closest to the camera. These men are probably from the 82nd Airborne, which was not as keen on facial camouflage as the 101st Airborne. (MHI)

C-47s pass over the ships of Task Force U after their runs over Normandy. These are probably from the glider serials that delivered the gliders around dawn on D-Day. (NARA)

the west, since a secondary mission of his unit was to link up with the 82nd Airborne Division that was scheduled to land near Ste Mère-Église. In doing so, a company became engaged in a series of encounters with German infantry around the village of Fournel that lasted through much of D-Day. The 1/502nd PIR held the northern perimeter throughout D-Day without serious challenge from the Germans except at Fournel.

US AIRBORNE LANDINGS, 6 JUNE 1944

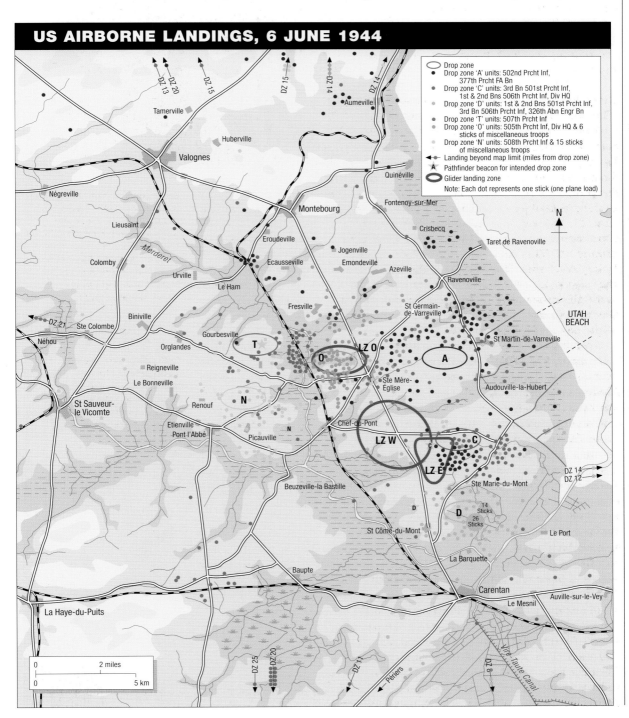

Drop zone
● Drop zone 'A' units: 502nd Prcht Inf, 377th Prcht FA Bn
● Drop zone 'C' units: 3rd Bn 501st Prcht Inf, 1st & 2nd Bns 506th Prcht Inf, Div HQ
● Drop zone 'D' units: 1st & 2nd Bns 501st Prcht Inf, 3rd Bn 506th Prcht Inf, 326th Abn Engr Bn
● Drop zone 'T' units: 507th Prcht Inf
● Drop zone 'O' units: 505th Prcht Inf, Div HQ & 6 sticks of miscellaneous troops
● Drop zone 'N' units: 508th Prcht Inf & 15 sticks of miscellaneous troops
◄ Landing beyond map limit (miles from drop zone)
▲ Pathfinder beacon for intended drop zone
⬭ Glider landing zone
Note: Each dot represents one stick (one plane load)

Of all the units in this sector, the 377th Parachute Field Artillery, with 12 75mm pack howitzers, was the most badly dispersed with some even landing near the marshes around St Marcouf, and others far north around Valognes. This meant there was no artillery fire support in this sector except for a single howitzer.

The southern sector was the responsibility of the two battalions of the 506th PIR, landing in Drop Zone C. The cloudbank disrupted the C-47s, and some aircraft passed over a concentration of German flak near Etienville; six aircraft were shot down and 30 damaged. In spite of the fire, some drops were concentrated, with one serial of 14 aircraft dropping almost on top of Drop Zone C and another serial of 13 bunching their sticks a mile and a half east and southeast of the drop zone. But the other serials were much further from their intended targets due to confusion over the beacons. About 140 men of the HQ and 1/506th PIR assembled in the regimental area in the first hours of the landing, including the regimental commander, Colonel Sink.

The 2/506th PIR landed north of the drop zone in the same area as the 501st PIR, but Lieutenant Colonel Robert Strayer managed to collect about 200 men by 03.30hrs. Strayer's group began moving south to seize the areas behind the Houdienville (Exit 2) and Pouppeville (Exit 1) causeways. Sink had no idea where Strayer's men had landed, and so instructed the assembled paratroopers of Lieutenant Colonel William Turner's 1/506th PIR to take control of the Pouppeville (Exit 1) causeway. Strayer's men were delayed by persistent German small arms fire and did not arrive at the Houdienville (Exit 2) causeway until early afternoon, by which time the access road had already been overrun by troops from the 4th Infantry Division moving inland. Turner's column also had tough going and it took several hours to reach the Poupeville (Exit 1) causeway.

Paratroopers of the 101st Airborne cluster around a Renault UE armored tractor that had been impressed into service to help carry supplies from the drop zone to the "Stopka strongpoint" near Ravenoville on D-Day. The troops with the circle insignia on their helmets to the left are from the divisional artillery while the paratrooper in the center with the white spade insignia is from the 506th PIR. (NARA)

Next to land were the 3/501st PIR and the divisional HQ, which was to control the planned glider-landing area near Hiesville. The 3/501st PIR lost three aircraft to flak on the approach. A force of about 300 paratroopers from the HQ and Lieutenant Colonel Julian Ewell's 3/501st PIR congregated near Hiesville. General Taylor, not knowing what was happening with Strayer's and Turner's two columns, decided to ensure that the southernmost Poupeville causeway was under US control, and so dispatched Colonel Ewell with 40 of his men around 06.00hrs. This was the first of the three paratrooper columns to actually reach the causeway around 08.00. The 2./GR.919 manned the WN6 strongpoint covering the western end of the causeway and WN2a on the beach itself. The defenses were poorly organized, but it took nearly four hours for the outnumbered paratroopers to overcome the German defenders in house-to-house fighting. The Germans surrendered around noon after suffering 25 casualties; 38 surrendered and the remainder who tried to escape across the causeway toward strongpoint WN2a on the beach were captured by advancing infantry of the 4th Division. About half of Ewell's men were casualties, but they made contact with the 2/8th Infantry at Exit 1.

Fighting flared up near the divisional CP in Drop Zone C due to the presence nearby of troops from Artillery Regiment.191 centered around Ste Marie-du-Mont. The paratroopers gradually eliminated the batteries, and the town was finally cleared of German troops by mid-afternoon when they were reinforced by GIs from the 8th Infantry advancing from the beaches.

The final groups to land were the 1/501st PIR, elements of the 2/501st PIR, the 3/506th PIR as well as engineer and medical personnel. These forces were earmarked for Drop Zone D, the southernmost of the drop zones. The approach to the drop zone was hot, with a considerable amount of light flak, searchlights, and magnesium flares. Six C-47s were shot down and 26 damaged. These drops were among the most successful in putting the paratroopers near their intended objective, but this was not entirely fortuitous, as the Germans had assumed that this area could be used for airborne landings. As this was the last of the divisional landings, the German troops in the sector were alerted and had troops near the landing zone. The 1/501st PIR commander was killed and his executive

A patrol from the 101st Airborne tows supplies from the drop zone on D-Day. The paratrooper to the right has used a captured German belt to carry a pair of German "potato masher" hand-grenades while one of his comrades carries what appears to be a German officer's service cap. (NARA)

officer captured. The regimental commander, Colonel Johnson, landed near the center of the zone and was able to rally about 150 paratroopers. He immediately set off for the primary objective, La Barquette locks controlling the flooding of the areas along the Douve River. The force brushed aside the German sentries and occupied the locks, but was soon under fire from German artillery. With the situation at the locks in hand, around 09.00hrs Johnson and about 50 paratroopers returned to the landing zone to seek reinforcements. About half of 2/501st PIR was engaged in a sharp firefight around the village of Les Droueries, and had been unable to disengage and move south to the objective. Instead of encountering the single platoon expected in this sector, they were confronted by an entire battalion, III/GR.1058. They spent most of the day fighting around the town of St Côme-du-Mont. Johnson was able to collect a few additional paratroopers and set off to seize or destroy the bridges over the Douve River below its junction with the Merderet River.

The third unit landing in Drop Zone D, the 3/506th PIR, had the roughest time. German troops were waiting in the landing area and had soaked a wooden building with fuel. They set the building on fire, illuminating the descending paratroopers. The battalion commander and his executive officer were among those killed in the first moments. Captain Charles Shettle, the battalion S-3, landed away from the main drop zone and set off to the le Port bridge with about 15 men. This small group gradually increased in size as it attracted scattered paratroops, and emplaced itself at two of the bridges by 04.30hrs. They were forced back by German counterattacks around 06.30hrs as they were nearly out of ammunition. However, they took up positions near the bridges, and were able to keep the Germans at bay. Ironically, the next day Shettle was able to call in a P-47 strike in hopes of attacking the German positions, but due to confusion, the P-47s skip bombed the bridges instead.

A pair of 82nd Airborne paratroopers from the 505th PIR eye a rabbit, though it is unclear whether they view it as a potential pet or potential lunch. This photo was taken near Ste Mère-Église on D-Day and provides some details of the paratroopers specialized garb including the jump gloves and scarves made from camouflage fabric. (NARA)

A patrol of paratroopers from the 508th PIR, 82nd Airborne move through the churchyard of St Marcouf on D-Day. (NARA)

BOSTON MISSION

The 82nd Airborne Division revised its plans on 28 May due to the discovery that the 91st Luftlande Division had moved into its planned landing area. The 82nd Airborne's new assignment was to land two regiments on the western side of the Merderet River, and one regiment on the eastern side around Ste Mère-Église to secure the bridges over the Merderet. The landings of the 82nd Airborne were even more badly scattered than those of the 101st Airborne and as a result, only one of its regiments was able to carry out its assignment on D-Day. The 82nd Airborne began landing about an hour after the 101st Airborne, around 02.30hrs.

The 505th PIR was assigned to land on Drop Zone O to the northwest of Ste Mère-Église. Unlike many other transport serials, those flying to Drop Zone O spotted the cloudbank early and managed to fly over it in coordinated fashion. The only cloud problems were over the drop zone itself, forcing some C-47 pilots to initiate the drop higher than usual at 1,000 feet. The pathfinders had done such a thorough job marking it that many aircraft circled back over the area to drop the paratroopers more accurately. This was the most precise series of jumps of any that night. Lieutenant Colonel Edward Krause's 3/505th PIR was assigned to take the town of Ste Mère-Église and managed to assemble about 180 paratroopers. The town had been garrisoned by the supply element of the divisional anti-aircraft unit Flak Regiment Hermann, but most of the 200 men of the unit left the town before the arrival of the paratroopers. Krause ordered his men into the town with explicit instructions to limit their actions to knives, bayonets and grenades to make it easier to distinguish German defenders. Krause's group quickly seized the town, killing about 10 German troops and capturing 30 others.

Lieutenant Colonel Benjamin Vandervoort's 2/505th PIR collected about half its troops and set out to establish a defense line north of the drop zone as planned. However, at 09.30hrs, the German GR.1058 staged a counterattack against Ste Mère-Église from the south. The regimental commander, Colonel William Ekman, ordered Vandervoort to return back southward to assist in the defense. Before doing so, he broke off a platoon to remain at Neuville and carry out the battalion's original mission. It proved to be a crucial decision. Shortly after establishing a defensive perimeter north of the town, Lieutenant Turner Turnbull's platoon was hit by a German infantry company but managed to hold his position during an eight-hour struggle. Only 16 of the 44 paratroopers in Turnbull's platoon survived the fighting, but the platoon's defense shielded the battalion while it faced an even greater threat to the south.

The 2/505th PIR arrived in Ste Mère-Église around 10.00hrs and took over part of the perimeter defense. The first German attack consisted of two companies from the Georgian Battalion 795 and troops of the 91st Luftlande Division with a few of the division's StuG IIIs. It was repulsed by the 3/505th PIR. Colonel Krause ordered a counterattack and about 80 men from Company I advanced southward along the road, hitting one of the retreating German convoys with a grenade attack. This was the one and only German attack of the day against the town.

The 1/505th PIR landed with the headquarters including General Ridgway. Around 04.00hrs, Company A under Lieutenant John Wisner set off for the La Fière bridge with about 155 paratroopers. This group increased in size as it approached the bridge, picking up stragglers from the 507th and 508th PIR. The advance on the bridge was slowed by frequent encounters with German troops. An initial attempt to rush the bridge failed due to entrenched German machine-gun teams, the first of several attempts that day in a confusing series of engagements.

The two other regiments of the 82nd Airborne Division landing in Drop Zones T and N on the west side of the Merderet River were hopelessly scattered. Pathfinders had been unable to mark the drop zones, in some

Another view of a group of paratroopers from the 508th PIR near the church in St Marcouf on D-Day. The sergeant in the foreground is armed with the folding-stock version of the M1 carbine, developed for the airborne forces. (NARA)

This 88mm Flak 36 anti-aircraft gun was one of a battery of four captured by the 82nd Airborne in Normandy. It appears to have been spiked with its breech removed. (MHI)

cases due to the proximity of German troops. The transport aircraft were disrupted by the coastal cloudbank, and after arriving over the drop area, the pilots had searched in vain for the signals, or in some cases homed in on the wrong beacon. Much of the 507th PIR was dropped into the marshes east of Drop Zone T while the 508th was dropped south of Drop Zone N. These swamps were deep and many of the heavily laden paratroopers drowned before they could free themselves of their equipment. In addition, a great deal of important equipment and supplies landed in the water, and valuable time had to be spent trying to retrieve this equipment. About half of the 508th PIR landed within two miles of the drop zone, but the remainder landed on the other side of the Merderet River or were scattered to even more distant locations. The 507th PIR dropped in a tighter pattern than the 508th, but many aircraft overshot the drop zone, dumping the paratroopers into the swampy fringes of the Merderet River. The most noticeable terrain feature in the area of the 507th PIR drop was the railroad line from Carentan on an embankment over the marshes. Many paratroopers gathered along the embankment.

La Fière Bridge

One of the missions of the 507th PIR was to seize the western approaches to the La Fière bridge, which connected the drop zones west of the Merderet River with Ste Mère-Église and the paratroopers on the east side. The bridge was a small stone structure over the Merderet River, but the farmland on the west side of the river had been flooded by the Germans to prevent its use as an airborne landing zone. The connection between the bridge and the hamlet of Cauquigny over the flooded area was a long, tree-lined causeway.

After the first attempt by Lt Wisner of A/505th PIR to rush the bridge, the eastern approaches became a collection point for paratroopers trying to make their way to the west side of the Merderet River, having been wrongly dropped on the eastern side. By mid-morning about 600 para-

This modest little stone bridge over the Merderet River at La Fière was the scene of some of the fiercest fighting on D-Day by the 82nd Airborne Division. This photo was taken by Gen Gavin after the fighting. (MHI)

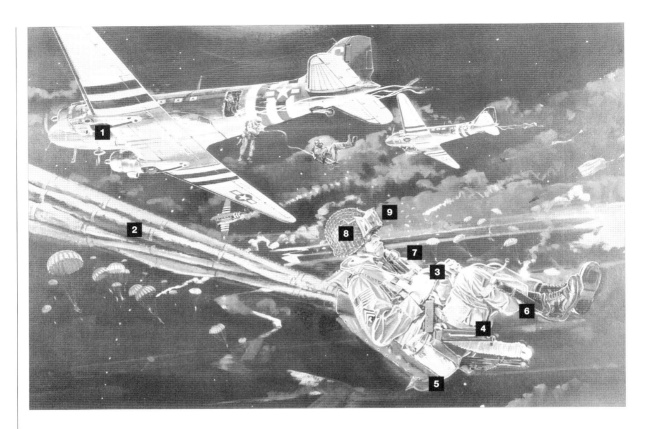

BOSTON MISSION – 82ND AIRBORNE DIVISION OVER DROP ZONE T, 02.40HRS, D-DAY (pages 38–39)

Based at Fulbock in England, the 442nd Troop Carrier Group was attached to the 52nd Wing for the D-Day airlift. The group's four squadrons made up Serial 26 of Mission Boston and arrived over Drop Zone T between 02.39 and 02.42hrs on D-Day. The serial carried 45 sticks of paratroopers: 36 from the rifle companies of the 1st Battalion, 507th Parachute Infantry Regiment, and 9 sticks of the headquarters company. The group lost one aircraft on the approach to the drop zone, and suffered damage to 31 of its aircraft due to flak over the drop zone. This shows aircraft from the 305th Troop Carrier Squadron (TCS), which carried the codes 4J on the nose (1) (the other squadrons were J7: 303rd TCS; V4: 304th TCS; 7H: 306th TCS). The C-47 was a military derivative of the Douglas DC-3 civil airliner. The main structural difference between the two types was the use of a large cargo door on the left rear side of the C-47 fuselage. The C-47 had simple, folding bench seats in the main cabin instead of conventional passenger seats. On paratrooper missions such as this, the typical load was one "stick" of paratroopers, which usually totalled 18 to 20 paratroopers. Alternatively, fewer paratroopers and more carge could be air-dropped. The paratrooper in the foreground, a Tech 5 from the 507th Parachute Infantry Regt. (PIR), is seen moments after jumpng from the aircraft. After leaving the C-47, the aircraft's slipstream tended to blow the paratrooper backward and curl him up. As the static line opened up the T-5 parachute pack,

the olive drab canopy began to deploy (2). The large surface of area of the deploying canopy tended to swing the paratrooper around again, and within seconds, the shroud lines cleared the pack and the canopy blossomed, giving the paratrooper a hard jolt. Quick deployment of the parachute was essential since the drops were conducted from only 700 feet. US paratroopers also carried a reserve chute on their chest (3). This paratrooper is armed with a .45 cal. Thompson sub-machine gun (4), which has been tucked under the waist web of the T-5 parachute harness to keep it in place. The paratroops carried a good deal of equipment into combat. Just visible under the harness is his yellow "Mae West" life vest. His musette bag hangs under the reserve chute, an ammunition bag from his right hip (5), and an assault gas mask in waterproof bag from his left hip (not visible). He has a fighting knife (6) strapped to his right leg above his jump boots. Although not visible here he also carries a .45 cal automatic in a holster on his hip with a folding knife in its scabbard in front of this. On his chest is a TL122C flashlight (7). Paratroopers on D-Day wore the M1942 paratroop battledress with its distinctive pockets. The paratrooper's M1C helmet (8) resembles the normal GI helmet, but has a modified liner and chinstrap to absorb the shock of the opening parachute. The first aid packet (9) taped to the front of the helmet for ready access contained a field dressing, tourniquet and morphine. Many paratroopers wore gloves to protect their hands during the jump.
(Howard Gerrard)

troopers had coalesced and a force under Captain F. "Ben" Schwarzwalder from the 2/507th PIR began a house-to-house skirmish to clear the manor farm on the eastern side of the bridge. When General Gavin arrived later, he split the growing force, sending a team of 75 paratroopers south to find another crossing point, while leading a second group of 75 to the bridge at Chef-du-Pont. General Ridgway arrived afterwards, and ordered Colonel Lindquist of the 508th PIR to organize the various groups near La Fière and capture the bridge.

Unknown to the force on the east side of the La Fière bridge, about 50 paratroopers of the 2/507th PIR had attempted to cross the bridge earlier in the morning from the western side. After being forced back by machine-gun fire, they established a defensive position in the Cauquigny church on the other end of the causeway. The attack against the bridge from the east side began around noon and about 80 paratroopers under Schwarzwalder pushed over the causeway and linked up with the platoon on the western side. Schwarzwalder's men were not followed by any other troops, and he decided that they should join up with the rest of their battalion under Lieutenant Colonel Charles Timmes in an orchard in Amfreville to the northwest of Cauquigny. Schwarzwalder left behind about a dozen paratroopers, believing they would be adequate to hold the bridge until other paratroopers from the east side passed over. However, before the force on the eastern side moved more paratroopers across, GR.1057 of the 91st Luftlande Division attacked with the support of a few Hotchkiss H-39 light tanks of Panzer Abteilung 100, quickly regaining control of the western side of the causeway in Cauquigny. As a result, the bridgehead over the Merderet was lost for the next two days and would be the scene of intense fighting.

The group under General Gavin that split off to seize the Chef-du-Pont bridge had no success. The bridge was stubbornly defended by a small number of German troops dug in along the causeway. Gavin's force was ordered back to La Fière to reinforce the main effort, and he left behind an understrength platoon commanded by Captain Roy Creek to cover the bridge. This unit was nearly overwhelmed by a later German counterattack, but they were rescued in the nick of time by the unanticipated arrival of a glider carrying a 57mm anti-tank gun, followed by reinforcements from La Fière. The reinforcements allowed Creek's force to clear the Germans off the bridge and cross the river to the west side.

A glider train passes over the French coast on the afternoon of D-Day, part of the re-supply missions. One of the German strongpoints is evident below in the center of the photo. (NARA)

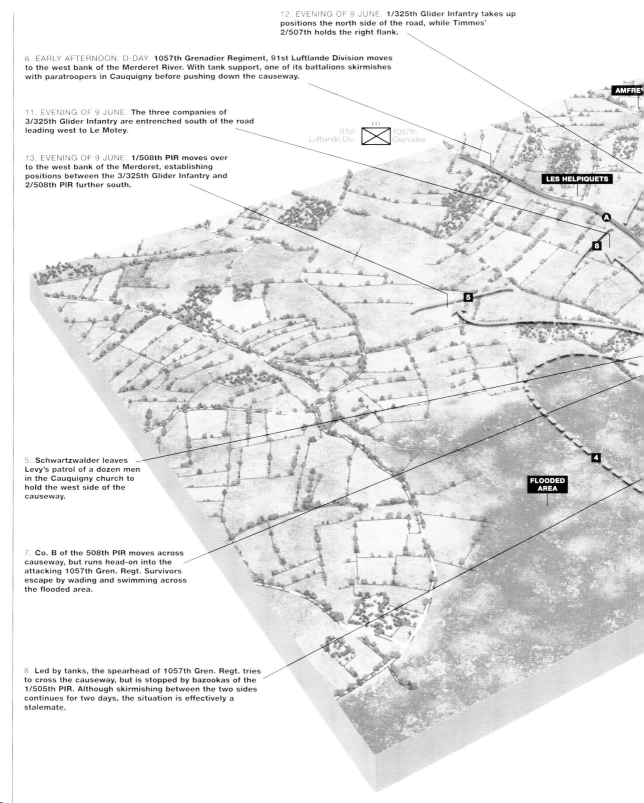

12. EVENING OF 9 JUNE. **1/325th Glider Infantry takes up positions the north side of the road, while Timmes' 2/507th holds the right flank.**

6. EARLY AFTERNOON, D-DAY. **1057th Grenadier Regiment, 91st Luftlande Division moves to the west bank of the Merderet River. With tank support, one of its battalions skirmishes with paratroopers in Cauquigny before pushing down the causeway.**

11. EVENING OF 9 JUNE. **The three companies of 3/325th Glider Infantry are entrenched south of the road leading west to Le Motey.**

13. EVENING OF 9 JUNE. **1/508th PIR moves over to the west bank of the Merderet, establishing positions between the 3/325th Glider Infantry and 2/508th PIR further south.**

91st
Luftlande Div. |X| 1057th
Grenadier

AMFRE

LES HELPIQUETS

A

8

5

4

FLOODED AREA

5. Schwartzwalder leaves Levy's patrol of a dozen men in the Cauquigny church to hold the west side of the causeway.

7. Co. B of the 508th PIR moves across causeway, but runs head-on into the attacking 1057th Gren. Regt. Survivors escape by wading and swimming across the flooded area.

8. Led by tanks, the spearhead of 1057th Gren. Regt. tries to cross the causeway, but is stopped by bazookas of the 1/505th PIR. Although skirmishing between the two sides continues for two days, the situation is effectively a stalemate.

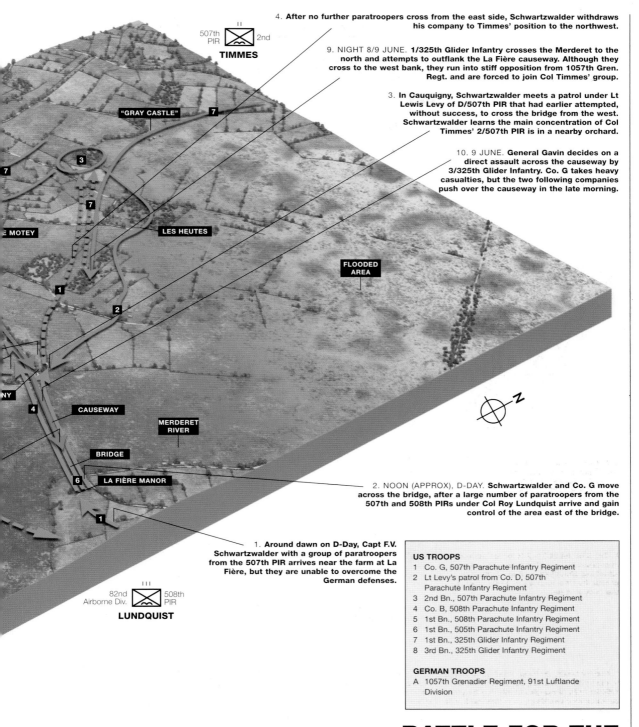

4. After no further paratroopers cross from the east side, Schwartzwalder withdraws his company to Timmes' position to the northwest.

507th PIR 2nd

TIMMES

9. NIGHT 8/9 JUNE. 1/325th Glider Infantry crosses the Merderet to the north and attempts to outflank the La Fière causeway. Although they cross to the west bank, they run into stiff opposition from 1057th Gren. Regt. and are forced to join Col Timmes' group.

3. In Cauquigny, Schwartzwalder meets a patrol under Lt Lewis Levy of D/507th PIR that had earlier attempted, without success, to cross the bridge from the west. Schwartzwalder learns the main concentration of Col Timmes' 2/507th PIR is in a nearby orchard.

"GRAY CASTLE" 7

3

7

7

7

E MOTEY

LES HEUTES

FLOODED AREA

10. 9 JUNE. General Gavin decides on a direct assault across the causeway by 3/325th Glider Infantry. Co. G takes heavy casualties, but the two following companies push over the causeway in the late morning.

1

2

N

NY

4 CAUSEWAY

MERDERET RIVER

BRIDGE

6 LA FIÈRE MANOR

1

2. NOON (APPROX), D-DAY. Schwartzwalder and Co. G move across the bridge, after a large number of paratroopers from the 507th and 508th PIRs under Col Roy Lundquist arrive and gain control of the area east of the bridge.

1. Around dawn on D-Day, Capt F.V. Schwartzwalder with a group of paratroopers from the 507th PIR arrives near the farm at La Fière, but they are unable to overcome the German defenses.

82nd Airborne Div. 508th PIR

LUNDQUIST

US TROOPS
1 Co. G, 507th Parachute Infantry Regiment
2 Lt Levy's patrol from Co. D, 507th Parachute Infantry Regiment
3 2nd Bn., 507th Parachute Infantry Regiment
4 Co. B, 508th Parachute Infantry Regiment
5 1st Bn., 508th Parachute Infantry Regiment
6 1st Bn., 505th Parachute Infantry Regiment
7 1st Bn., 325th Glider Infantry Regiment
8 3rd Bn., 325th Glider Infantry Regiment

GERMAN TROOPS
A 1057th Grenadier Regiment, 91st Luftlande Division

BATTLE FOR THE LA FIÈRE BRIDGE, MERDERET RIVER

6–9 June 1944, viewed from the southeast, showing the bitter 4-day struggle for the La Fière Bridge. This small bridge and its associated causeway over the Merderet River proved crucial in the early operations beyond Utah Beach as they were the main link between the separated elements of the 82nd Airborne Division.

One of the few other coherent operations of the early morning on the west bank of the Merderet involved a force assembled by Lieutenant Colonel Thomas Shanley of the 2/508th PIR near Picauville. His unit's assignment was to destroy the Douve bridge at Pont l'Abbé, but his force quickly came in to contact with a German infantry battalion from GR.1057 involved in sealing off the west bank of the Merderet River. Shanley withdrew his force to the battalion assembly area on Hill 30 and they fought a day-long engagement, shielding the operations of the forces near La Fière.

By the afternoon of D-Day, there were three separated groups of paratroopers in the area around La Fière bridge: about 300 paratroopers with Shanley, 120 with Timmes and Schwarzwalder, and 400 with Col George Millett of the 507th PIR on the east side of La Fière. All three groups were short on ammunition, and under intense pressure from GR.1057. As will be detailed later, the fighting for La Fière continued for three days.

Glider Reinforcements

The next airborne missions in the early hours of D-Day were the glider reinforcement flights: Mission Detroit for the 82nd Airborne Division and Mission Chicago for the 101st Airborne Division. Mission Detroit left England at 01.20hrs with 52 Waco C-4A gliders carrying 155 troops, 16 57mm anti-tank guns, and 25 jeeps. One of these gliders, carrying the division's SCR-499 long-range radio, was lost shortly after take-off. A second aircraft and glider were lost before reaching Landing Zone E. The overloaded glider carrying the 101st Airborne deputy commander,

Table 2: D-Day Glider Operations, IX Troop Carrier Command

Mission	Chicago	Detroit	Keokuk	Elmira	Galveston	Hackensack	Total
Mission date	D-Day 04.00	D-Day 04.07	D-Day 21.00	D-Day 21.00	D+1 07.00	D+1 09.00	
Landing zone	LZ E	LZ O	LZ E	LZ W	LZ W	LZ W	
Tow aircraft sorties	52	52	32	177	102	101	516
Aborted sorties	1	0	0	2	2	0	5
Aircraft lost or missing	1	1	0	5	0	0	7
Aircraft damaged	7	38	1	92	26	1	165
Horsa sorties	0	0	32	140	20	30	222
Horsa sorties aborted	0	0	0	2	2	0	4
Waco sorties	52	53	0	36	84	70	295
Waco sorties aborted	1	1	0	0	2	0	4
Aircrew killed or missing	4	4	0	1	0	0	9
Aircrew wounded	1	3	0	8	0	0	12
Glider pilots dispatched	104	106	64	352	208	200	1,034
Glider pilots lost	14	13	0	26	0	3	56
Troops carried	155	220	157	1,190	968	1,331	4,021
Troops landed	153	209	157	1,160	927	1,331	3,937
Waco casualties*	27	30	0	15	35	16	123
Horsa casualties*	0	0	44	142	80	74	340
Artillery carried	16	16	6	37	20	0	95
Vehicles carried	25	27	40	123	41	34	290
Cargo carried (tons)	14	10	19	131	26	38	238

*troops injured or killed during landing

Landing in twilight in small, congested farm fields, many gliders like this Waco CG-4A made very rough landings. Although there had been hopes to retrieve and reuse the gliders after Normandy, most were damaged beyond repair. (MHI)

Brigadier General Donald Pratt, crashed on landing, killing the general. The nighttime landings at 03.45hrs were almost as badly scattered as the paratroopers with only 6 gliders on target, 15 within three-quarters of a mile, 10 further west and 18 further east. Nevertheless, casualties were modest with five dead, 17 seriously injured and seven missing.

The 46 Waco CG-4A gliders of Mission Detroit landed at 04.10hrs near the 82nd Airborne's Landing Zone O, carrying 220 troops as well as 22 jeeps and 16 anti-tank guns. About 20 of the gliders landed on or near the landing zone, while seven were released early (five disappearing) and seven more landed on the west bank of the Merderet River. The rough landings in this sector led to the loss of 11 jeeps and most of the gliders, but troop losses were less than expected, 3 dead and 23 seriously injured.

THE GERMAN REACTION

German forces on the Cotentin peninsula were not on alert on the night of 5/6 June 1944 due to the weather conditions mentioned earlier. The first hint of activity came into German intelligence around 23.00–24.00 on 5 June when signals units picked up a coded message to French resistance. Around 23.30hrs, an aircraft warning station at Cherbourg alerted the local command that ship activity and the concentration of transport aircraft at British airfields suggested an invasion was underway. This set in train a number of alerts. The first news of paratroop jumps began arriving at headquarters around 01.30hrs from the area around the Vire River. These alerts increased in number through the early morning hours. One of the sticks of pathfinders landed on top of the regimental headquarters of GR.919, located in a quarry on the road between Quineville and Montebourg. Oberstleutnant Gunther Keil commanded the battalions along the coastline, and found a map on one of the paratroopers that indicated that the main drop would be around Ste Mère-Église. At first, the regimental headquarters believed that the paratroopers were part of a raid, and not a major drop. The Georgian Battalion.795 located east of Ste Mère-Église reported around 03.00hrs that the battalion was surrounded, but Keil was a bit skeptical as the messengers had arrived at the command post without difficulty and an

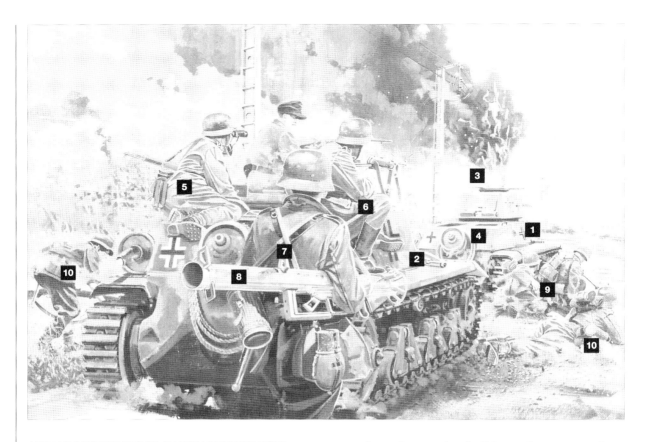

GERMAN COUNTERATTACK ON THE MERDERET RIVER,
14.00HRS D-DAY (pages 46–47)

Around 13.00hrs Grenadier Regiment.1057 of the
91st Luftlande Division began a counterattack towards the
La Fière causeway through Cauquigny. A company of
Hotchkiss H-39 tanks of PzAbt.100 spearheaded the attack,
but two were disabled in the first attack, which was beaten
off. The surviving pair of Hotchkiss tanks again took up the
lead, accompanied by infantry. Company A, 1/505th PIR had
set up a defensive position on the east side of the La Fière
bridge and earlier in the morning the paratroopers had placed
a string of anti-tank mines in plain sight on top of the road as
a deterrent to the Panzers. The Hotchkiss tanks sped ahead of
the accompanying infantry, and approached to within 40 feet
of the mines. The paratroopers had two bazooka teams in
ambush position and they immediately hit the first tank (1).
The second tank (2) had no room to maneuver on either side
of the causeway, and backed away. An infantry attack by
GR.1057 followed, which was stopped by small arms fire and
the support of some 60mm mortars. Attacks continued
through the day, with the paratrooper positions pounded by
German artillery. During a truce late in the day to recover the
wounded, a paratrooper surveyed the German positions on
the causeway and estimated they had suffered about
200 casualties in their brave but futile counterattacks. The
paratroopers had also taken heavy losses, and few of the men
holding the east side of the bridge survived D-Day. Around
02.00hrs on 7 June, the second Hotchkiss returned and
attempted to push the derelict tank off the road, but was
attacked in the dark by Sgt William Owens with Gammon

grenades, and retreated again. This was the last attempt by
Grenadier Regiment.1057 to cross the Merderet, but they
established blocking positions on the causeway that
prevented the paratroopers from crossing as well. The
Hotchkiss H-39 tank, dubbed "PzKpfw 38H 735(f)" in
Wehrmacht service, was a French cavalry tank captured in
the wake of the 1940 campaign. They were widely used by
the Wehrmacht in secondary roles, especially anti-partisan
fighting and saw combat in Finland, Yugoslavia, Russia, and
France. The Wehrmacht made several changes to the tanks,
most evidently cutting off the top of the turret cupola and
replacing it with a split hatch (3) for the tank commander.
After being rebuilt in 1941, they were repainted in standard
German dark gray, but many were camouflaged later with
the newer dark yellow color (4). Despite its name, the 91st
Luftlande Division was a regular army (Heer) division. As a
result, its uniforms were typical of those worn by the German
army in the summer of 1944. The Unteroffizier (NCO) (5),
riding on the back of the rear tank, is the squad leader (gruppen-
führer) and is armed with the ubiquitous 98k rifle, although
nominally the squad leader should be armed with a machine
pistol. His binoculars and map case set him apart from the
rest of the rifle squad. The soldier alongside him on the tank
is equipped with an MP40 machine pistol (6). Following the
tank is a richtschütze (7) armed with a Panzerschreck
anti-tank rocket launcher (8). A loader, not visible here, would
normally accompany him carrying two more rockets. The rest
of the squad includes the machine-gun team (9), consisting of
a gunner and assistant gunner and armed with a MG-42 light
machine-gun, and two more riflemen (10). (Howard Gerrard)

officer of the Georgian battalion arrived safely by car. He gave more credence to a report from a company of the divisional engineers who reported that thousands of paratroopers were landing.

At 84th Corps headquarters, Gen Marcks became concerned that the paratroopers might create a gap between the 709th Division at Utah Beach and the 352nd Division at Omaha. The only major corps reserve was Kampfgruppe Meyer of the 352nd Infantry Division near St Lô. At 03.10, Gen Marcks ordered Meyer to advance towards the junction of the two divisions between Utah and Omaha beaches. The decision to send the reserves after the paratroopers proved to be premature and a serious mistake. Later in the morning, the force would be badly needed in the opposite direction. As a result, Kampfgruppe Meyer spent most of the morning marching westward, only to have their orders changed a few hours later and shifted in the opposite direction, all the while under air attack.

US paratroopers landed mainly in the deployment area of the 91st Luftlande Division. The reaction of the division was confused, in part due to the absence of senior divisional commanders at the Rennes wargame. General Falley was alerted to the paratrooper landings early in

the morning and set out by car to return to his unit. Around dawn, his car was intercepted before reaching his command post by a paratrooper patrol and he was killed after a short skirmish near Picauville. Unaware of Falley's fate and unable to contact him, the division's operations officer, General Bernhard Klosterkemper, took temporary command. On learning that the Americans had seized Ste Mère-Église, he ordered GR.1057 to begin to move east over the Merderet via the La Fière bridge, where the regiment would become entangled with the 82nd Airborne Division over control of the Merderet River crossings.

In the meantime, Oberst Keil had asked permission from 84th Corps headquarters to use Major Moch's battalion from GR.1058 of the 91st Luftlande Division located at St Côme-du-Mont to assist him in his own efforts to regain control of Ste Mère-Église from the north. Permission was granted by corps HQ at 03.30hrs and Keil hoped that Moch's battalion would arrive at Ste Mère-Église by 08.00. Instead of moving on the town, Moch's battalion was still in its garrison north of Ste Mère-Église at 08.00hrs and Keil again ordered him to attack the town, without result. Finally, around 11.00hrs, Moch sent a message indicating that the battery at Azeville had been captured and asking Keil if he should retake it. At the end of his patience, Keil told him to follow the previous orders but Moch's battalion did not reach the outskirts of the town until 13.00hrs. By the afternoon, a perimeter defense had already been established and Moch's battalion reinforced the units assaulting Lt Turnbull's platoon outside Neuville, but were unable to overcome the outnumbered but tenacious paratroopers.

The German troops south of Ste Mère-Église, including the remnants of the Georgian Battalion.795, were pressed into a pocket by the paratrooper attacks from the north, and the advance of 4th Division troops from the beaches later in the day. This pocket continued to block the road south of Ste Mère-Église through D-Day.

While Moch's battalion was sluggishly approaching Ste Mère-Église, the corps headquarters ordered a second battalion from GR.1058 to follow it southward to the town. However, it became bottled up around Montebourg. The corps headquarters also activated the Sturm-Battalion

AOK 7 and sent it along the road from St Floxel to Beuzeville-au-Plain, eventually attacking the US positions on the eastern side of Ste Mère-Église in the afternoon. Elements of the Panzerjäger Company.709 accompanied it, but were lost in the fighting with the paratroopers around Beuzeville-au-Plain.

Fallschirmjäger Regiment.6 (FJR 6) near Periers was alerted around midnight, and began encountering paratroopers who had landed far south of the intended landing areas. Von der Heydte tried reaching higher command but telephone lines in the area had been cut, probably by the French resistance. The 3./FJR 6 engaged in skirmishes with US paratroopers in the pre-dawn hours, being pushed to the southeast. Von der Heydte finally managed to reach Gen Marcks around 06.00hrs by using phones at the St Lô post office, and he was ordered to clear the Carentan area of paratroopers and begin moving his regiment northward toward Ste Mère-Église with the objective of eliminating the paratrooper concentrations there. In the days prior to the invasion, Rommel had ordered units in areas vulnerable to paratroop landing to disperse their garrison, and as a result, FJR 6 had a difficult time assembling its troops. Von der Heydte passed through Carentan ahead of his troops, finding the town devoid of German or American troops, and he reached a German battalion dug in near St Côme-du-Mont. He climbed the village church's steeple, giving him a vista of the battlefield all the way to Utah Beach. The vast armada of US ships was clearly visible, and he later recalled that the scene was oddly tranquil, like a summer's day on the shore of the Wannsee near Berlin with little evidence of fighting. This was the first time that a senior German officer learned that the paratrooper attack had been reinforced by a major amphibious landing. As 3./FJR 6 was still engaged with US forces, the other two battalions reached this assembly area in the early afternoon. The 2./FJR 6 was directed to advance on Ste Mère-Église along the main road while the 1./FJR 6 would advance further east to shield the column from US troops landing from the sea. The two advancing battalions moved out around 19.00hrs and had no serious contact with US forces until after nightfall, when both battalions were heavily disrupted by further airborne landings virtually on top of them.

The fate of the I./GR.919 stationed along Utah Beach was not recorded in detail due to its quick rout. Communications between the battalion and the division headquarters were lost before noon on D-Day as US troops captured most of its strongpoints. Of the 13 strongpoints, WN1 to WN14 along the coast, all of the southern strongpoints closest to the US landings were taken by US forces on D-Day. Those further north on the coast including WN10, WN10a, WN11 and StP12 held out for another day or two, finally surrendering after running out of food and ammunition.

THE AMPHIBIOUS LANDINGS

Task Force U under Rear Admiral Don Moon reached the transport area off Utah Beach around 02.30hrs and the command ship, USS *Bayfield*, dropped anchor. There was no significant German naval activity in the area even though Admiral Krancke had issued orders to repel the invasion force after shore radar had located the oncoming invasion fleet at 03.09hrs. Two torpedo boat flotillas operating out of Cherbourg encountered heavy seas, and returned to port before dawn without engaging the Allied landing force. The first actions of the day began around 05.05hrs when German coastal batteries began to open fire on Allied shipping as it crossed the horizon. The Morsalines battery of 6./HKAA.1261 with six French 155mm guns had been located in concrete emplacements near St Vaast, but due to air attacks, was moved to open ground near Videcosville. It began engaging a minesweeper, prompting HMS *Black Prince* to respond. The Marcouf battery of 3/HKAA.1261 and the neighboring 4/HKAA.1261 engaged the destroyers USS *Corry* and *Fitch*. While maneuvering to avoid the fire, the *Corry* struck a mine amidships, cutting it in two. The destroyers *Fitch* and *Hobson* pulled alongside while keeping the coastal batteries under fire. The Marcouf battery was subjected to the most intense fire, first by the cruiser *Quincy* and then by the battleship USS *Nevada*. *Nevada* scored a direct hit on one of the four bunkers with a 5in. round, but it was a dud, passing through the bunker and out the other side. The battery lost the first of three guns in the early morning exchange, the second at 15.57 and the last at 18.30hrs.

The preliminary naval bombardment of the beach began at H-40 (05.50hrs). As H-hour approached, the fire was redirected toward flank targets, especially remaining German naval batteries in the area. Utah Beach was scheduled for a preliminary air bombardment by IX Bomber Command. Although cloud cover threatened to

The 14in. guns of the battleship USS *Nevada* begin pounding German fortifications along Utah in preparation for the landings. One of the principal missions of the naval gunfire support was to eliminate the numerous German coastal batteries north of Utah Beach. (NARA)

In contrast to Omaha Beach where the heavy bomber attacks were completely ineffective, the attacks on Utah by B-26 Marauder medium bombers substantially disrupted the W5 strongpoint. These are B-26 bombers of the 553rd BS, 386th "Crusaders" Bomb Group and they display the white and black invasion stripes on their wings and fuselages. (NARA)

disrupt the bombardment, the attacking B-26 Marauder pilots decided to drop below the prescribed altitude to 3,500–7,000 feet. A total of 269 bombers took part, dropping 525 tons of 250lb bombs between 06.05 and 06.24hrs. This was in complete contrast to Omaha Beach where the bombers remained above the cloud cover, and ineffectively dropped their bombs far behind the beach using blind-bombing tactics. Besides the bombardment of the beach itself, a further 33 aircraft dropped 47 tons of bombs on the coastal artillery batteries near Maisy and Gefosse.

The preliminary bombardment proved to be extremely effective in suppressing the German defenses at the WN5 strongpoint. Most of the open gun pits had been knocked out by the attacks, and even some of the enclosed bunkers had collapsed or were seriously damaged. One of the few defense positions intact was the well-protected Bauform 667 casemate on the southern fringe of WN5. Although casualties from the bombardment had been low, many of the German defenders were stunned by the bomb blasts and naval gunfire.

The first landing actually occurred two hours before the main landings. Activity had been spotted on the St Marcouf islands off Utah Beach in May, so a cavalry detachment of 132 men from the 4th and 24th Cavalry Squadrons were sent ashore at 04.30hrs. In fact, there were no German troops on the islands, but minefields and later German artillery fire killed two and wounded 17.

As on Omaha Beach, the preliminary force ashore was scheduled to be amphibious Duplex Drive M4A1 medium tanks. The 32 tanks from the 70th Tank Battalion were carried toward their launch point on board eight LCTs. The run toward the beach was slowed by the headwind and steep chop. At 05.21hrs, one of the two control craft guiding in the force

An aerial view of Utah Beach taken on D-Day. The area behind the beach was flooded, and beyond that, the *bocage* typical of Normandy can be seen. (NARA)

1. **06.30HRS.** The first wave lands at H-Hour consisting of 20 LCVPs carrying four companies of the 8th Infantry: Companies E and F land on Uncle Red Beach, Companies B and C on Tare Green.

2. **06.40HRS.** The first assault wave is followed by eight LCTs carrying two companies of 32 M4A1 DD amphibious tanks. Although they are supposed to land before the infantry, in the event, they are delayed reaching the start line and arrive on the beach some ten minutes after the infantry.

3. **06.35HRS.** The second assault wave at H+5 carries the remainder of the 8th Infantry in 32 LCVPs. This consists of companies G and H on Uncle Red and Companies A and D on Tare Green. This wave also includes the navy and engineer demolition teams to remove beach obstructions.

4. **06.45HRS.** The third wave at H+15 consists of Company C, 70th Tank Battalion, with their M4 and M4A1 tanks fitted with deep-wading trunks. This company also includes the battalion's dozer-tanks that are assigned to help the engineers in clearing beach obstructions.

5. **06.47.** The fourth wave, landing at H+17 consists of eight LCMs and three LCVPs bringing ashore the engineers to help complete the removal of beach obstructions between the high water and low water marks. A detachment from the 237th Engineer Battalion lands on Uncle Red while the 299th lands on Tare Green.

9. The neighboring German strongpoint, WN3, is located 1,300 yards away; too far to offer any covering fire to WN5. It is attacked and cleared later in the morning by 2/8th Infantry with few casualties.

13. **09.00HRS.** The bulk of the two assault battalions of 8th Infantry Regt. attempt to exit the beach via the causeway.

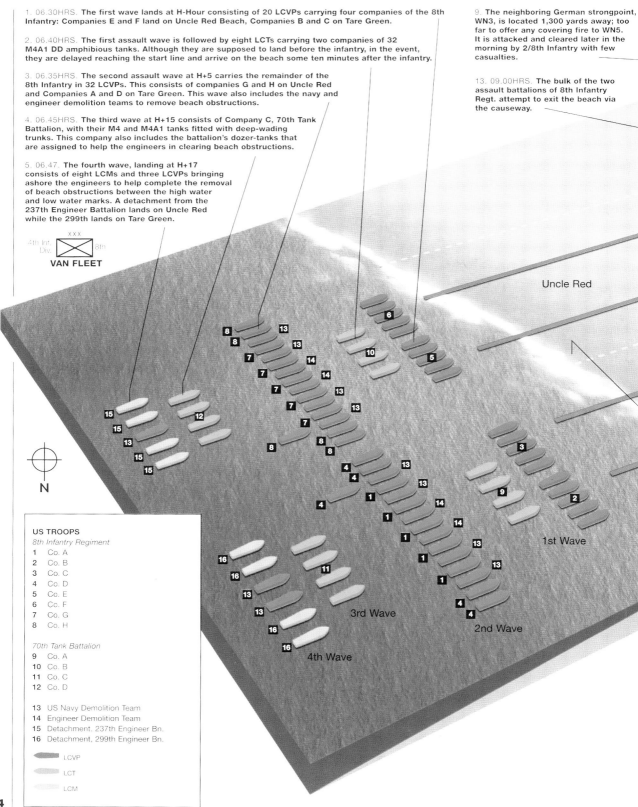

4th Inf. Div. XXX 8th
VAN FLEET

N

Uncle Red

1st Wave

2nd Wave

3rd Wave

4th Wave

US TROOPS

8th Infantry Regiment
1 Co. A
2 Co. B
3 Co. C
4 Co. D
5 Co. E
6 Co. F
7 Co. G
8 Co. H

70th Tank Battalion
9   Co. A
10 Co. B
11 Co. C
12 Co. D

13 US Navy Demolition Team
14 Engineer Demolition Team
15 Detachment, 237th Engineer Bn.
16 Detachment, 299th Engineer Bn.

LCVP
LCT
LCM

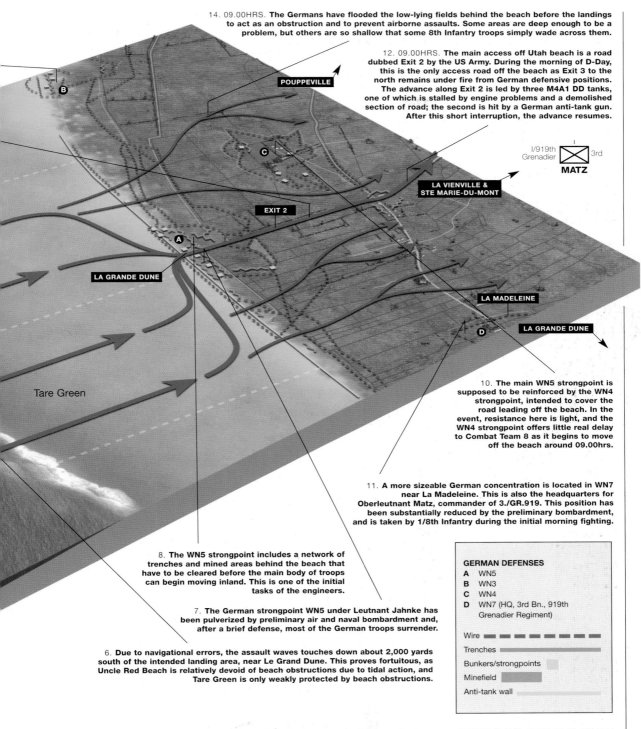

14. 09.00HRS. The Germans have flooded the low-lying fields behind the beach before the landings to act as an obstruction and to prevent airborne assaults. Some areas are deep enough to be a problem, but others are so shallow that some 8th Infantry troops simply wade across them.

12. 09.00HRS. The main access off Utah beach is a road dubbed Exit 2 by the US Army. During the morning of D-Day, this is the only access road off the beach as Exit 3 to the north remains under fire from German defensive positions. The advance along Exit 2 is led by three M4A1 DD tanks, one of which is stalled by engine problems and a demolished section of road; the second is hit by a German anti-tank gun. After this short interruption, the advance resumes.

POUPPEVILLE

I/919th Grenadier — 3rd
MATZ

LA VIENVILLE & STE MARIE-DU-MONT

EXIT 2

LA GRANDE DUNE

Ⓐ

Ⓑ

Ⓒ

Ⓓ

LA MADELEINE

LA GRANDE DUNE

Tare Green

10. The main WN5 strongpoint is supposed to be reinforced by the WN4 strongpoint, intended to cover the road leading off the beach. In the event, resistance here is light, and the WN4 strongpoint offers little real delay to Combat Team 8 as it begins to move off the beach around 09.00hrs.

11. A more sizeable German concentration is located in WN7 near La Madeleine. This is also the headquarters for Oberleutnant Matz, commander of 3./GR.919. This position has been substantially reduced by the preliminary bombardment, and is taken by 1/8th Infantry during the initial morning fighting.

8. The WN5 strongpoint includes a network of trenches and mined areas behind the beach that have to be cleared before the main body of troops can begin moving inland. This is one of the initial tasks of the engineers.

7. The German strongpoint WN5 under Leutnant Jahnke has been pulverized by preliminary air and naval bombardment and, after a brief defense, most of the German troops surrender.

6. Due to navigational errors, the assault waves touches down about 2,000 yards south of the intended landing area, near Le Grand Dune. This proves fortuitous, as Uncle Red Beach is relatively devoid of beach obstructions due to tidal action, and Tare Green is only weakly protected by beach obstructions.

GERMAN DEFENSES

A	WN5
B	WN3
C	WN4
D	WN7 (HQ, 3rd Bn., 919th Grenadier Regiment)

Wire	▬ ▬ ▬ ▬ ▬ ▬
Trenches	▬▬▬▬▬▬▬
Bunkers/strongpoints	▮
Minefield	▬▬▬▬
Anti-tank wall	▬▬▬▬▬▬▬

ASSAULT WAVES, COMBAT TEAM 8, UTAH BEACH

06.30–09.00hrs, 6 June 1944, viewed from the north. As a result of the offshore current and poor visibility, Combat Team 8's first wave lands 2,000yds south of the intended landing zone. The defenses are less formidable and the assault actually easier. The German strongpoints are rapidly overcome and the troops push inland to link up with troops from the 82nd and 101st Airborne.

struck a mine and sank, followed 15 minutes later by an LCT. The naval control officer realized that the force was behind schedule, and to speed the landing, the LCTs launched the tanks from closer to shore than planned, from about 1,500 yards (1,300m) instead of 5,000 yards (4,550m). Even so, the 28 DD tanks arrived ten minutes after the first wave of troops.

The assault force for Utah Beach was Combat Team 8, formed from the 8th Infantry of the 4th Infantry Division, along with supporting engineers and other specialist troops. The initial two waves consisted of two assault battalions, more heavily equipped than normal infantry, landing in LCVPs. The first wave included 20 LCVPs with 30 troops each. The offshore current pushed the craft somewhat to the south, and the landmarks on shore were difficult to see due to the smoke caused by the heavy bombardment. As a result, the first wave of the assault force landed about 2,000 yards (1,800m) south of the intended objective around Exit 3 and Les Dunes de Varreville, landing instead near Exit 2 and the Grande Dune. The navigational error had little effect on the operation, and if anything permitted an easier landing as it transpired that there were fewer beach obstructions in this sector and the German strongpoints were less substantial. Instead of facing two major German strongpoints on the intended beach, the landing faced only a single strongpoint that had been pulverized by the aerial bombing. Several company-sized task forces set about reducing the German strongpoints along the beach, which was accomplished without difficulty aided by the newly arrived DD tanks. The tanks quickly knocked out the surviving bunkers, and began breaching the seawall using gunfire. The commander of the German defenses, Leutnant Jahnke, ordered the Goliath remote control vehicles to be launched against the tanks and landing craft, but the bombardment had severed the wire guidance cables to their hidden nests.

German resistance on Utah Beach was quickly overwhelmed except for sporadic artillery shelling from distant coastal batteries. This view from a Coast Guard LCVP shows troops wading ashore with an LCI beached to the left. The barrage balloons were intended to prevent low-altitude strafing by German aircraft.

Company C of the 70th Tank Battalion goes ashore at Utah Beach in the third wave. The first two companies of the 70th Tank Battalion used DD tanks, while this company used deep-wading trunks. (NARA)

Tank casualties on Utah Beach were due almost entirely to mines. This M4 medium tank named "Cannonball" of Co. C, 70th Tank Battalion became trapped in a hidden shell crater while driving to the beach from its LCT. The two deep-wading trunks are very evident in this view. (NARA)

The first assault wave was followed by 32 more LCVPs containing the remainder of the two assault battalions along with engineer and naval demolition parties. The demolition teams set about destroying beach obstructions to permit the landing of additional craft once the tide had turned. The engineers began to tackle the problem of minefields along the beach, and also used explosive charges to blow gaps in the seawall to allow the troops speedier passage off the beach. The third wave at H+15 consisted of 8 more LCTs containing Company C from the 70th Tank Battalion using M4 tanks fitted with wading trunks as well as four dozer-tanks to assist in the beach-clearing operation. The fourth wave consisted mainly of detachments from the 237th and 299th Engineers to assist in clearing the beaches. Two additional battalions, 3/8th Infantry and 3/22nd Infantry also followed. By this stage, German fire was limited to sporadic artillery. Most of the German defenders surrendered quickly, but Jahnke was not pulled from his command bunker until around noon during the clean-up operations.

The first senior officer on the beach was General Theodore Roosevelt Jr., the 4th Division's assistant commander. On realizing they had landed on the wrong beach, he personally scouted the exits to determine which causeway to use to exit the beach. Roosevelt met with the two infantry battalion commanders and instructed them to eliminate remaining German defenses and move out over the Exit 2 causeway. By 09.00hrs, the defenses behind the beach had been reduced and the 8th Infantry was moving inland, led by tanks from the 70th Tank Battalion. On the way down the causeway, the Germans had set off a demolition charge under a small culvert, creating a gap in the road. The lead tank had mechanical problems, stalling the second tank, which was struck by an anti-tank gun. The third tank quickly eliminated the gun and engineers from the Beach Obstacle Task Force brought up a length of treadway bridge to cover the gap. Due to congestion on the causeway, some units moved across the flooded tidal pools behind the beach.

The 1/8th Infantry moved north from the causeway and reached Turqueville by evening without encountering any serious resistance. The

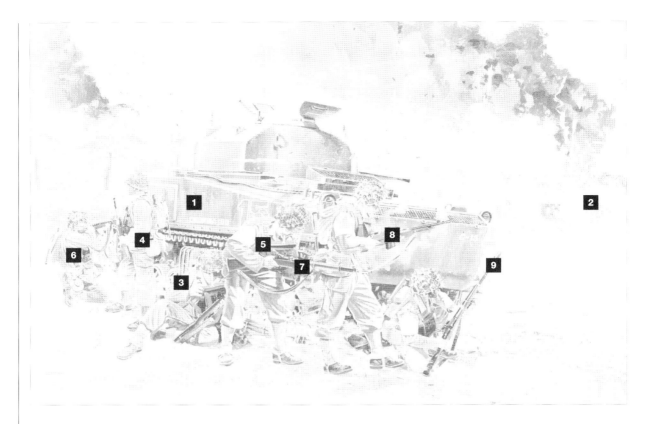

COMBAT TEAM 8 ON UTAH BEACH, 07.30HRS D-DAY
(pages 58–59)

The M4A1 Sherman tanks of Company C, 70th Tank Battalion arrived on Utah Beach in the third wave aboard LCTs at H+15. Unlike the battalion's two other companies of tanks fitted with **DD Duplex Drive** equipment, which in theory at least allowed them to "swim" ashore, Company C relied on deep-wading trunks to get to the beach. After reaching the shoreline, the crew detached the clumsy upper trunks, but the lower adaptor trunks are still evident on this tank. The mission of the tanks on the beach was to help the infantry in overcoming any beach defenses, and to assist in exiting the beach by blasting the seawall with their guns. Here "Colombia Lou" (1), one of the company's M4 medium tanks, engages a German Bauform 667 bunker (2) with GIs from the 8th Infantry (3) taking cover behind the advancing tank. These ferro-concrete bunkers were so thick that naval gunfire or bombs could not easily knock them out. The only effective method to silence them was to engage them at relatively close quarters, firing directly into the bunker's embrasure. Assault troops of the 8th Infantry wore distinctive battledress on D-Day. Due to the suspicion that the Germans might use chemical weapons to defeat the landings, the troop's uniforms were impregnated with a solution that prevented the chemical agent from soaking into the clothing. On Omaha beach, the usual battledress was impregnated with this chemical preparation. On Utah Beach, the assault troops wore a set of chemically impregnated HBT (herringbone tweed) battledress (4) over their normal uniforms. They could then discard the HBTs after the landings. The black waterproof bag (5) they are carrying contains an assault gas mask. Another item specially developed for the D-Day landings was the assault vest (6), which was intended to take the place of normal webbing, ammunition pouches, and musette bags all in a single garment. In the event, the assault vest proved to be cumbersome and unworkable and the concept was discarded. All the members of the fire team seen here are armed with the M1 Garand rifle (7) except for one team member who is armed with a BAR (Browning Automatic Rifle) (8). The GI on the right has a rifle grenade adapter fitted to his rifle (9), and is preparing to fire a rifle grenade at the German defenses. Due to the recoil from launching these grenades, the prescribed method of firing them was to place the butt of the rifle on the ground.
(Howard Gerrard)

3/8th Infantry headed directly west from the causeway, and ran into elements of the 14th Company of GR.919, the regimental anti-tank unit, with a platoon of 75mm anti-tank guns deployed in field positions along with infantry from the I./GR.919. A short firefight ensued in which about 50 Germans were killed and about 100 surrendered. The battalion reached the area north of Les Forges and sent out a platoon to link up with the 82nd Airborne Division near Chef-du-Pont. The 2/8th Infantry headed south toward Pouppeville along the seawall rather than crossing the causeway. There was almost continuous skirmishing with isolated German riflemen along the coast, but the battalion overwhelmed the weakly defended WN2a strongpoint and made their way to Exit 1 and the road junction near Pouppeville. They linked up with Colonel Ewell of the 3/501st PIR who had already cleared the town of troops from GR.1058. Besides the actions by the 8th Infantry, A/49th Engineer Combat Battalion was assigned to seize a lock near Grand Vey that controlled the flooding of the tidal pools. In the process, they took about 125 German prisoners.

The remainder of the 4th Infantry Division landed on D-Day, along with the first elements of the 90th Division. Both the 12th and 22nd Infantry were directed toward the northern side of the beachhead area. Starting from a position further south than the planned landing area, they did not reach their objectives on D-Day. They formed a defensive perimeter emanating westward from St Germain-de-Varreville towards Ste Mère-Église.

Reinforcement of the airborne divisions continued through the day. Howell Force, a reserve of troops from 82nd Airborne Division under Colonel E. Raff, landed by sea and followed 3/8th Infantry, planning to join up with their parent unit. On reaching the area near Les Forges where the 3/8th Infantry had set up its nighttime bivouac, Raff was told that the infantry planned to advance no further that night as they were already in possession of their objective and had run into German defenses north of their position. Raff wanted to link up with airborne forces in Ste Mère-Église, and was also concerned about the safety of Landing Zone W, the destination of Mission Elmira, another glider supply effort. Attempts to budge the German defenses had not succeeded by the time that the gliders appeared over the landing zone around 21.00hrs, and the fields were in no-man's land. The first wave consisted of 54 Horsa and 22 Waco CG-4A gliders with 437 troops, 64 vehicles, 13 57mm anti-tank guns and 24 tons of supplies. In the declining light, the gliders landed under fire from scattered German positions. The main hazard was the difficulty of landing the gliders in confined farm fields at dusk, and many gliders crashed on landing. The casualties were surprisingly light considering the circumstances. The second wave of the Elmira mission consisting of 86 Horsa and 14 Waco CG-4A gliders landed about an hour and a half later in Landing Zone O north of Ste Mère-Église. The third and smallest glider landing of the evening, Operation Keokuk, crunched into Landing Zone E, west of Hiesville.

D-Day at Midnight

By midnight on D-Day, Utah Beach was securely in American hands and the 4th Infantry Division had reached its initial objectives, at a very modest cost, only 197 casualties. The startling contrast in the casualties compared to the more than 2,000 suffered on neighboring Omaha Beach were due to the weak defenses on Utah Beach and the total disruption of German defenses by the airborne landings. Omaha Beach was defended by 11 strongpoints instead of the one at Utah, and the defending forces there had 26 anti-tank guns and field guns aimed at the beach compared to only 5 at Utah Beach. There was a similar discrepancy in machine-guns and mortars. In addition, the Utah Beach bunkers were heavily damaged by the preliminary bombardment, while the Omaha bunkers were never bombed. Utah Beach was defended by only about a company of infantry, while Omaha Beach had portions of two infantry regiments. Tanks also

The W5 strongpoint at Utah Beach had a French 47mm Model 1937 anti-tank gun among its defenses that was knocked out by the preliminary bombardment. The Wehrmacht made extensive use of captured equipment in its Normandy defenses as well as older German equipment deemed obsolete for the Russian front. (NARA)

A view of Utah Beach after the initial landings. The most common anti-tank defensive work at Utah Beach was the Bauform 60 50mm anti-tank gun pit seen to the right. There were about 1,800 of these guns used for coastal defense in 1944. (NARA)

This 50mm anti-tank gun in the Bauform 667 casemate was knocked out by a direct hit on its shield by tank gun fire. These ferro-concrete bunkers were nearly impervious to bombing and naval gunfire, and had to be eliminated by close combat assault. (USAOM)

landed in force on Utah, with nearly three intact companies on the beach in the opening hour of the fighting.

The air landings by the 82nd and 101st Airborne Divisions had not gone according to plan, due to dispersion of the drops. Only about ten per cent of the paratroopers landed on their drop zones, a further 25 per cent within a mile, and another 20 per cent within two miles. The remainder were more scattered: about 25 per cent were within five miles, 15 per cent were between five and 25 miles from their drop zones, and about five per cent were missing. By dawn, the 82nd Airborne Division had only about 1,500 paratroopers near their divisional objectives and the 101st Airborne had only about 1,100. By midnight, the situation was not much better, only about 2,000 under divisional control with the 82nd and 2,500 with the 101st Airborne Division of the 13,350 dropped. While the serious dispersion accounts for the problems in the morning, the continued difficulties collecting troops during the course of the day was due to the unexpected isolation of small groups of paratroopers by the maze of hedgerows and flooded farmlands and the lack of sufficient radios to link the dispersed groups. Casualties sustained by the airborne units on D-Day have never been accurately calculated as so many troops were missing for days afterwards. Nevertheless, it is evident that casualties in these units were considerably higher than those suffered by the 4th Infantry Division during the beach landings. Indeed, total casualties in the Utah sector were comparable to the 2,000 casualties on Omaha Beach, but a significant portion of these casualties were paratroopers captured by the Germans and non-combat injuries sustained during the night drops.

As a result of the difficulties in assembling the paratroopers, the objectives of the airborne divisions were not met on D-Day. The airborne divisions did secure some of the access routes off the beach, but the

As the 8th Infantry began exiting Utah Beach over the Exit 2 causeway, one of the DD tanks from Co. A, 70th Tank Battalion was hit by a hidden anti-tank gun. The damaged tank was pushed off the causeway to clear it for following troops. As can be seen, the canvas flotation screens on this DD tank had been folded down. (MHI)

only causeway that really mattered was seized by the 8th Infantry. Bridges over the Merderet were not secured, and large portions of the 82nd Airborne remained cut off on the west side of the river. Equally worrisome, the airborne divisions did not manage to create an effective defensive screen on the southern edge of the VII Corps lodgment, leaving the bridgehead vulnerable to attack by German reserves. This had no consequence due to the weak German response.

By the perverse logic of war, the airborne assault actually did accomplish its mission even if specific objectives were not achieved. The paratroopers were so widely scattered that they disrupted and tied down most German forces on the eastern side of the Cotentin peninsula. If the US airborne commanders were unhappy over their failures, the German senior commanders were baffled. Some German officers believed that the airborne assault represented a clever new tactical approach they dubbed "saturation attack", intended to disrupt defensive efforts by the German army rather than to control specific terrain features. Although the Germans may have been impressed by the airborne landings, senior Allied leaders were not. The problems with the Normandy landings convinced them that nighttime landings were inherently too risky given the limitations of contemporary navigation technology, and subsequent Allied airborne operations were conducted in daylight.

German defensive operations on D-Day had been passive and unsuccessful. The vaunted Atlantic Wall in this sector had been breached within an hour with few casualties. The combat performance of German infantry units, not surprisingly, was quite mixed. Some units, such as GR.1057 along the Merderet, attacked and defended with tenacity and skill. Many of the static defense units surrendered to the paratroopers even though they outnumbered the attackers, especially those with conscripted Poles and "volunteer" Soviet prisoners. In general, the Utah Beach sector received relatively little attention from German corps and army head-quarters due to the perception that other sectors were far more dangerous, especially the British beaches. Indeed, it was not apparent to senior German commanders until late in the day that a major amphibious landing was under way at Utah Beach.

Troops from the 8th Infantry wade through some of the inundated farm fields behind Utah Beach. The cylindrical devices the two lead GIs are carrying are their inflated floatation belts. These troops are also carrying the distinctive assault gas-mask bags so typical of the Normandy landings. (NARA)

CONSOLIDATING THE BEACHHEAD

General Collins, commander of VII Corps, realized that his first mission would be to consolidate the beachhead area due to the lingering dispersion of the paratroop forces. He was still not in touch with General Ridgway from the 82nd Airborne Div., and the first communications were not received until late on D+1. The primary mission of the day was to eliminate the German pocket south of Ste Mère-Église, and to relieve the pressure on the northern sector of the town's defenses. The pocket contained the remnants of the Georgian Battalion.795 and GR.919. By dawn, the 8th Infantry was poised along its southern and eastern flank, and

Fighting went on for several days to clear the German strongpoints along the coast north of Utah Beach. This is a sniper patrol from 3/22nd Infantry checking out a farm in the Dunes des Varreville area on 10 June 1944. (NARA)

The Georgian Battalion.795 Ost was stationed immediately behind Utah Beach and involved in the D-Day fighting. This Georgian captain was captured after their positions were overrun. Curiously enough, he had featured in a series of German propaganda photos taken before D-Day of Hitler's new allies. (NARA)

attacks began that morning. Although the Georgians resisted the initial attacks, a Russian-speaking GI was able to convince them to surrender. About 250 troops gave up to the 1/8th Infantry. The two other battalions of the 8th Infantry had a much harder fight against German units holding a ridge that covered the access road to Ste Mère-Église, but this was overcome, and the two battalions fought their way into town. In the meantime, Collins had already ordered a column of tanks of C/746th Tank Battalion to Ste Mère-Église along the eastern road, and these arrived in time to beat back an early afternoon attack by GR.1058, supported by StuG III assault guns. The 82nd Airborne was reinforced during the day by additional air-landings of the 325th Glider Infantry at 07.00 and 09.00hrs in the Les Forges area. Fighting continued around the La Fière bridge, with the paratroopers repulsing German attacks. But at the end of D+1, a substantial portion of the 82nd Airborne Div. remained cut off on the western side of the Merderet. Nevertheless, the fighting on D+1 solidified the 82nd Airborne positions on the eastern bank, with the division now in firm control of Ste Mère-Église and connected to the seaborne invasion force.

The other two regiments of the 4th Division pushed northward out of the beachhead along the coast. The most difficult fighting took place around the fortified German coastal gun positions at Azeville and Crisbecq. Although the two regiments were able to push about two miles northward during the day, they were unable to overcome the two fortified areas and suffered heavy casualties. The 3/22nd Infantry advanced along the coast and reduced the surviving German beach strongpoints. Naval fire-control parties helped direct the gunfire of warships against the bunkers. By the evening of D+1, the battalion had fought its way through all of the German defenses up to WN11 when it was ordered inland to serve as a reserve for the other two battalions of the 22nd Infantry that had been battered that day in the fighting with the coastal artillery fortifications. While moving across the inundated tidal flats westward, a German prisoner reported that most of his comrades in the WN13 strongpoint wanted to surrender after a day of pounding from naval gunfire. As a result, the 3/22nd Infantry swung behind WN11 and occupied WN13 further to the north, leaving behind a company to prevent the garrison of WN11 from escaping. This strongpoint surrendered the following day.

The 101st Airborne Div. was involved for most of D+1 in securing the southern flank of the beachhead, especially around St Côme-du-Mont and the Douve River north

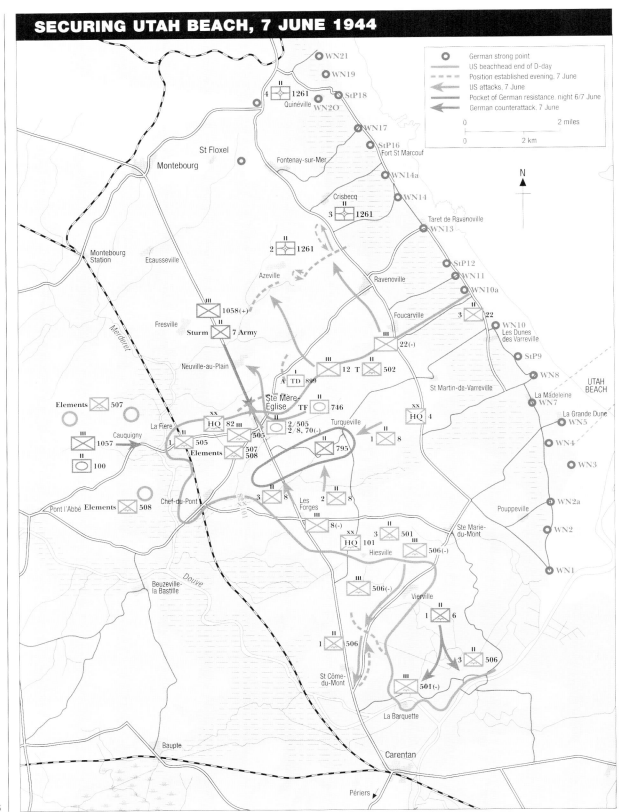

Legend:
- German strong point
- US beachhead end of D-day
- Position established evening, 7 June
- US attacks, 7 June
- Pocket of German resistance, night 6/7 June
- German counterattack, 7 June

0   2 miles
0   2 km

N

WN21
WN19
StP18
4   1261
Quinéville
WN2O
WN17
StP16
Fort St Marcouf
St Floxel
Montebourg
Fontenay-sur-Mer
WN14a
WN14
Crisbecq
3   1261
Taret de Ravenoville
WN13
Montebourg Station
Ecausseville
StP12
WN11
WN10a
2   1261
Azeville
Ravenoville
Fresville
1058(+)
Foucarville
3   22
Sturm   7 Army
22(-)
WN10
Les Dunes des Varreville
Neuville-au-Plain
12 T   502
StP9
A TD 899
WN8
UTAH BEACH
St Martin-de-Varreville
Elements   507
Ste Mère-Église
La Mádeleine
WN7
TF   746
La Grande Dune
HQ 82
XX
HQ 4
WN5
La Fière
505
2/505
2/8, 70(-)
Turqueville
1   8
WN4
1057
Cauquigny
1   505
Elements
507
508
795
WN3
100
Chef-du-Pont
3   8
Les Forges
2   8
Pouppeville
WN2a
Pont l'Abbé   Elements   508
8(-)
3   501
Ste Marie-du-Mont
WN2
HQ 101
XX
Hiesville
506(-)
WN1
506(-)
Beuzeville-la Bastille
Vierville
1   6
1   506
3   506
St Côme-du-Mont
501(-)
La Barquette
Baupte
Carentan
Périers

Counterattacks by GR.1058 on the paratroopers in Ste Mère-Église included a number of StuG. III assault guns. This one was hit no fewer than four times, but from the size of the gouges on the bow, it was probably a victim of M4 tanks of the 746th Tank Battalion. An airborne 57mm anti-tank gun sits beside it. (MHI)

of Carentan. Two battalions of German paratroopers from FJR 6 had been advancing through this area on D-Day, with 1./FJR 6 reaching the area of Ste Marie-du-Mont and 2./FJR 6 reaching within a mile of Ste Mère-Église from the east. Von der Heydte, after seeing the scale of the American operation, realized that his attack on Ste Mère-Église with a mere two battalions was a fool's errand, and during the night of 6/7 June, ordered both battalions to withdraw. The 2./FJR 6 received the order and withdrew but the other battalion did not respond. It belatedly withdrew southward during D+1 toward the rear of the defensive positions of the 101st Airborne Division along the Douve River. It nearly bumped into a column from 1/506th PIR heading out of Vierville, but the American column hesitated to fire as the identity of the force was very unclear. By late afternoon, about 300 German paratroopers from the 1./FJR 6 began approaching the rear of Captain Shettle's force of about 100 paratroopers from 3/506th PIR. The American paratroopers responded with a series of aggressive patrols that convinced the Germans they were facing a much superior force. About 40 Germans were killed in the skirmishes, but platoon-sized units began surrendering, eventually totaling 255 men by evening, outnumbering their captors by a large margin. The remainder of the 1./FJR 6, numbering about 500 German paratroopers, began approaching the defensive perimeter held by 250 paratroopers under Colonel Johnson who were positioned near the La Barquette locks and the Le Port bridge. Not realizing that US forces held the area, the German paratroopers marched carelessly into an ambush and were halted by a blast of small arms fire at 350 yards. Skirmishing followed, and Johnson finally sent an ultimatum, ordering the Germans to surrender or be annihilated by his "superior forces". Small groups of German paratroopers began

A paratrooper patrol moves through the outskirts of Ste Mère-Église on 10 June, clearing out isolated groups of German stragglers still in the town. (NARA)

surrendering and by nightfall about 150 Germans had been killed or wounded, and another 350 surrendered at a cost of ten US paratroopers killed and 30 wounded. Only 25 German paratroopers survived the debacle and made it over the river to Carentan.

While this fighting was going on, other elements of the 101st Airborne were making their way toward St Côme-du-Mont in a series of small skirmishes with the Sturm-Abt. AOK 7 and elements of 3./FJR 6. By the end of the day, the force around St Côme-du-Mont included five airborne battalions, two artillery battalions and a company of light tanks. These would form the core of an assault force to strike south to the key town of Carentan to help link up Utah and Omaha beaches.

Although the VII Corps had made solid progress on D+1, it was still behind schedule. Under the original plan, Collins had hoped that the 4th Division could rapidly exit the beachhead and begin advancing north toward Cherbourg. However, the fighting was progressing much more slowly than hoped due to the inability of the 82nd Airborne Division to control the Merderet River crossings, the unexpected difficulties of infantry combat in the coastal hedgerows, and the three-day delay in consolidating the badly scattered paratroopers. During a visit to Normandy on D+1, Eisenhower expressed his concern to Bradley that the Germans might exploit the gap between the V Corps on Omaha Beach and the VII Corps on Utah. As a result, Bradley instructed Collins to focus his immediate attention on closing this gap by seizing Carentan.

Rommel had originally believed that the main Allied effort was on the Calvados coast, especially in the British sector around Caen.

Paratroopers from the 101st Airborne Division pass through Ste Marie-du-Mont on 12 June 1944. Aside from the divisional patches, the paratroopers can be distinguished from the regular infantry units by their distinctive battledress including the cargo pockets on their trousers. (NARA)

On 8 June he received a set of orders for the US VII Corps that had been found by a German unit near Utah Beach. This made it clear that the Allies intended to push northward out of Utah Beach toward Valognes and eventually take Cherbourg. As a result, he diverted a first-rate unit, the 77th Infantry Division, which had been intended to prevent the link-up of Omaha and Utah beaches, and ordered it instead into the Cotentin peninsula to reinforce the Cherbourg front. The task of preventing the link-up of the two American beaches in the Carentan sector was assigned to the new and inexperienced 17th SS-Panzergrenadier Division "Gotz von Berlichingen".

THE BATTLE FOR CARENTAN

The force attacking Carentan was placed under command of Brigadier General Anthony McAuliffe, better known for his later role in the defense of Bastogne. The plan was to seize St Côme-du-Mont, which controlled the highway to Carentan. The defense of Carentan fell mainly to the two surviving battalions of FJR 6 under Oberstlt von der Heydte. He gathered a number of withdrawing German infantry companies to the defense, and on 9 June the corps attached a further two Ost battalions, which he deployed on the eastern side of the town due to their dubious potential.

After a preliminary artillery preparation on the morning of 8 June, one glider infantry and three paratroop battalions began the assault. The survivors of Sturm-Abt. AOK 7 began to retreat out the west side of St Côme-du-Mont, but then veered southward toward the main road,

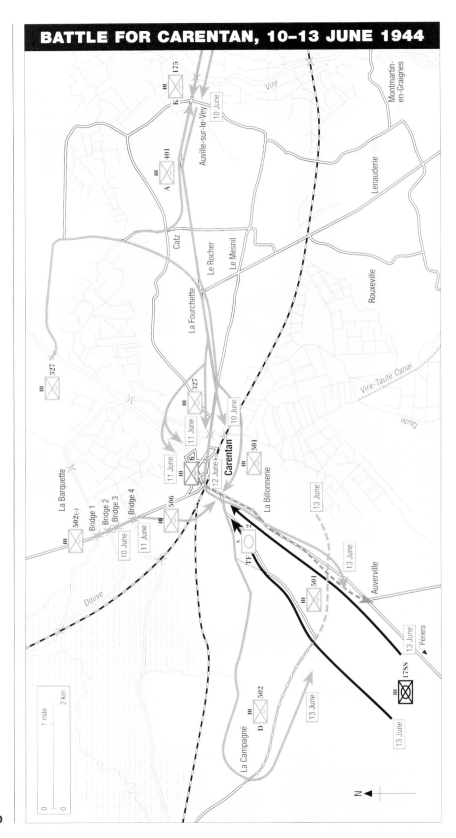

After von der Heydte's battered FJR 6 retreated out of Carentan, the 17.SS-Pz.Gren. Division tried to retake the town on 13 June 1944. In the foreground is a 57mm anti-tank gun of the 82nd Airborne while behind it to the right is one of the StuG IV assault guns of 1./SS-Pz.Abt. 17 that was knocked out during the fighting about 3.5km (2.2 miles) outside Carentan on the Periers road near the crossroads with the D223 leading to Baupte and La-Haye-du-Puits. The paratroopers used the light-weight airborne Mk. 3 version of the British 6-pdr instead of the standard US Army 57mm anti-tank gun. (NARA)

colliding with the 3/501st PIR. A series of skirmishes ensued that were finally settled when two more paratroop battalions pushed past the town. By the end of the day, McAuliffe's forces had gained control of the northern side of the causeway leading to Carentan over the Douve and Madeleine rivers. The nature of the fighting that ensued was determined by the terrain. The area on either side of the causeway consisted of marshes and flooded farmland that was mostly impassable to infantry. As a result, the fighting had to be conducted down the narrow causeway itself and across each of its four bridges. The retreating German force had blown the first bridge over the Douve River, and so the advance along the bridge did not begin until the night of 9/10 June while the engineers attempted to span the gap. A boat patrol that night reached as far as the fourth and final bridge over the Madeleine River, but came under intense fire from Carentan. An artillery barrage preceded the attack by the 3/502nd PIR in the early evening of 10 June. The battalion was stretched out in a thin column from the second to fourth bridge, when German machine-gunners began to open fire. Advance across the Madeleine River bridge was inhibited by a Belgian gate obstacle that the paratroopers had managed to move, creating a single 18in. gap. As a result, only one soldier at a time could pass over the bridge. The fighting continued after dark, and was marked by a strafing run by two Luftwaffe aircraft, a rare appearance in the Normandy skies.

By dawn, about 250 paratroopers had reached the final Madeleine bridge, which was overlooked by a stone farmhouse. At 06.15hrs, Col Cole and the battalion executive officer, Major John Stopka, led a bayonet charge by 70 paratroopers into the farm. Although the farm was taken, by this stage the 3/502nd PIR had taken such heavy casualties that the 1/502nd PIR was brought forward to carry on the attack. In fact, the position was so tenuous that the 1/502nd could do no more than reinforce Cole's men to hold the farm against repeated German counterattacks. An afternoon attack almost succeeded in overwhelming the US paratroopers, but an artillery barrage placed almost on top of the American positions broke the German attack. Around 20.00hrs, the 2/502nd PIR was brought forward to relieve the other two battered battalions. By now, von der Heydte's German paratroopers were beginning to show the strain of combat as well, experiencing serious shortages of machine-gun ammunition and receiving few reinforcements. All rifle ammunition was collected and turned over to the machine-gun crews, and the paratroopers were forced to rely on pistols, grenades or whatever else was at hand. A request to airlift small arms ammunition to the beleaguered garrison was granted on 11 June, but the drop zone was in a field nearly nine miles (14km) behind the front, taking time to collect and distribute.

During the two days of intense fighting by the 502nd PIR along the causeway, the 327th Glider Infantry had crossed the Douve further east in the early morning hours of 10 June. It was then reinforced by 1/401st Glider Infantry, which began moving south to seize the roads leading

The initial defenders of Carentan were Fallschirmjäger Regiment 6, which had already lost one of its battalions in the first days of fighting against the US paratroopers. This photo shows a team of German paratroopers on an exercise on 1 June 1944 shortly before the invasion, wearing their distinctive helmets. (MHI)

A GI inspects one of the StuG IV assault guns of SS-Pz.Abt. 17 knocked out along the Carentan–Periers road. This was a less common version of the standard German assault gun, based on the PzKpfw IV chassis. The ubiquitous StuG III was based on the PzKpfw III chassis. (NARA)

out of Carentan toward the east. One of its companies moved east toward Isigny, meeting up with scouts from the 29th Division, marking the first contact between Utah and Omaha beaches. By the end of 10 June, the 327th Glider Infantry set up a defensive perimeter covering the east side of Carentan, where it was joined by elements from the 401st Glider Infantry. In contrast to the frustrating assault over the causeway, this advance proceeded so well that McAuliffe ordered the 501st PIR to reinforce the glider infantry on 11 June in preparation for a final assault on 12 June. The situation of the German garrison had become so perilous that on the afternoon of 11 July, von der Heydte decided to withdraw his force rather than face certain annihilation. During a lull in the fighting in the late afternoon, the garrison began to slip out to the southwest.

The attack on the city in the early morning hours of 12 July consisted of a drive by the glider infantry from the northeast directly into Carentan and a pincer movement by the 501st and 506th PIR to cut the roads to the southwest to prevent the garrison from escaping. The city was captured quickly, but aside from a small rearguard, the garrison had already withdrawn. After Carentan was taken, the VII Corps set about reinforcing the connections with V Corps to the east.

As Von der Heydte's paratroopers made their way southwest from Carentan on 11 July, they bumped into the lead elements of the 17th SS-Panzergrenadier Division. Von der Heydte later claimed that he had not been informed of the reinforcement, but senior German commanders blamed him for the unauthorized and premature abandonment of the city after he had been informed several times about the plans. Generalleutnant Max Pemsel, the Seventh Army chief of staff, later wrote that von der Heydte had suffered a temporary mental and physical breakdown due to the savage and uninterrupted fighting of the previous several days. The only reason he was not relieved for such a "misguided" decision was the outstanding performance of his outnumbered regiment up to that point.

17.SS-Pz.Gren.Div. had been formed in November 1943, and was not complete when sent into action in June 1944. Although near strength in personnel, it had only about 60 percent of its officers and NCOs, and was very short of motor transport. The divisional commander, SS-Gruppenführer Werner Ostendorf, decided to retake Carentan by attacking down two roads on the western side of city. The attack would not be preceded by reconnaissance or artillery fire in order to gain tactical surprise, and would be spearheaded by SS-Panzer Abteilung 17 equipped with 48 StuG IV assault guns. Ostendorf felt that the sudden appearance of large numbers of armored vehicles would carry the day since, to date, the fighting in this sector had been conducted by light infantry on both sides with few anti-tank weapons. The Panzers would serve as the spearhead for the main attack by SS-Panzergrenadier Regiment 37.

McAuliffe had planned to deploy the 506th PIR into the same area on the morning of 13 June to deepen the defenses, but they had not begun to advance when the German attack began around 07.00hrs. The German columns started from the divisional assembly areas, and due to the congestion on the country roads, the advance was slow in progressing. No contact was made with the paratroopers until around 09.00hrs when the lead StuG IV assault guns had approached to within 875 yards (800m) of the southwestern side of Carentan. In the confined terrain southeast of the city, the 506th PIR was able to slow the attack by using the hedgerows to good effect. They were reinforced by the 2/502nd PIR on the right flank.

There had been growing indications from Enigma decryption that Rommel planned to deploy the 17th SS-Panzergrenadier Div. against Carentan, prompting Bradley to deploy a task force from the newly arrived 2nd Armored Division including a company of medium tanks, a company of light tanks, and an armored infantry battalion into the area. When the paratroopers reported the Panzer attack around 09.00hrs, the task force

The 90th Division began to move forward to replace the 82nd Airborne Division once the bridges over the Merderet had been cleared. This is a .30 cal machine gun team moving forward, the gunner in front with the .30 cal Browning light machine-gun, and his assistant behind carrying the tripod and ammunition. (NARA)

The 82nd Airborne was once again committed to action in mid-June to help speed the attack across the Contentin peninsula. This is Lt Kelso Horne, commander of 1st Platoon, Co. I, 508th PIR, near St Sauveur-le-Vicomte. (NARA)

began moving and reached the town around 10.30. The German attack petered out by noon. The inexperienced Panzergrenadiers had a hard time adjusting to the *bocage* fighting, and a combination of officer and NCO shortages as well as combat losses left many units leaderless. Some units began to retreat on their own, forcing von der Heydte and his adjutant to round up many of them, sometimes at gunpoint. The left flank of the German attack was supposed to be defended by the surviving Hotchkiss H-39 tanks of Panzer-Abteilung 100, but the battered force evaporated. The US armored counterattack began around 14.00hrs down the Carentan–Baupte road. This threatened to cut off the German attack force, especially when it was followed by a second tank–paratrooper thrust down the Carentan–Periers road. Von der Heydte, finding the SS-Panzergrenadier Regiment 37 commander dazed, took command and ordered the Panzergrenadiers as well as his force to withdraw to a line he had reconnoitered earlier. Losses in the 17th SS-Panzergrenadier Div were 79 killed, 316 wounded and 61 missing. In addition, only about half of the division's 48 StuG IV assault guns were still operational with seven lost, and 13 damaged.

Infuriated by the debacle, Ostendorf attempted to make von der Heydte the scapegoat for his division's failure, and had him arrested and sent before an SS military judge that night. General Meindl, in temporary command of this sector after General Marcks had been killed in an air attack the day before, ordered von der Heydte released. The Seventh Army staff concluded that the counterattack at Carentan had failed due to the 17th SS-Panzergrenadier Div.'s inexperience. The rebuff of the German counterattack allowed Collin's VII Corps to consolidate the link-up with Gerow's V Corps on 14 June.

A GI from the 9th Division, armed with a .45 cal Thompson sub-machine gun, moves along a shallow road embankment near St Sauveur-le-Vicomte during the effort to cut off the Cotentin peninsula. (NARA)

One of the more common German tank destroyers in the Normandy fighting was the Marder III Ausf. M, which consisted of the highly effective 75mm PaK 40 anti-tank gun mounted on the rear of the Czech PzKpfw 38 (t) tank chassis. This one from Panzerjäger Abt. 243 was captured by the 82nd Airborne Division during the fighting on the Cotentin peninsula. A knocked-out M4 medium tank can be seen ahead of it. (MHI)

CUTTING OFF THE COTENTIN

Although it had been Collins' intention to shift the emphasis of VII Corps to a rapid assault on Cherbourg, by D+3 the focus was changed again. The slow pace of the advance in the *bocage* convinced both Bradley and Collins that a quick capture of Cherbourg was unlikely. Under such circumstances, it became imperative to cut off the Cotentin peninsula from any further German reinforcements. The first issue was completing the link-up of the elements of the 82nd Airborne Division on either side of the Merderet River.

With the positions on the east bank of the Merderet at La Fière bridge secure, on D+1 Gavin sent the 3/508th PIR to Chef-du-Pont to link up with Col Shanley's isolated force on the west bank. The fire directed against the causeway during the daylight hours made it impossible to

LEFT **A fine character study of a typical young German *landser* of the 353rd Infantry Division during the Normandy fighting, wearing a shelter segment that doubled as a poncho. In front of him is his entrenching shovel and mess kit. This photo was taken on 25 June 1944 near La Haye-du-Puits during efforts by the Wehrmacht to prevent the American beachhead from pushing south out of the Cotentin peninsula. (MHI)**

RIGHT **GIs of the 9th Division use a roadside drainage ditch for cover during a skirmish near St Sauveur-le-Vicomte on 21 June 1944. In the background to the right is their 1¹/₂-ton weapons carrier while to the left is an abandoned German truck. (NARA)**

carry out this mission, though Shanley was able to send a patrol across the causeway at night.

On D+2, the focus again returned to La Fière bridge. On the night of 8 June, two paratroopers from Col Timmes' group found a partially submerged road across the inundated fields north of the bridge, and crossed to the east bank. A plan was developed for Colonel Millett's group to join Col Timmes' group, and then link up with a battalion from the east bank moving across the newly discovered crossing. Col Millett's column began moving before daylight on 9 June, but were discovered and raked by German machine-gun fire. Colonel Millett was captured and the column retreated. The 1/325th Glider Infantry was able to make it across the inundated river and join Timmes' group, but attempts to push southward to the La Fière bridge were repulsed by German troops in a stone building dubbed the "Gray Castle".

Under growing pressure from senior commanders, Gavin was forced to execute a direct assault across the La Fière causeway from the east bank. He moved a few M5A1 tanks and a company of the 507th PIR to the forward edge of the bridge to provide covering fire. The force chosen for the assault was the 3/325th Glider Infantry. After a preliminary artillery bombardment and under a partial cover of smoke, Company G led the attack off at 10.45hrs on 9 June. The glidermen were told to make the 500-yard crossing in one sprint, but only a handful of men were able to do so in the face of intense German machine-gun fire. Those who hesitated were caught in the open on the exposed stretches of the causeway, and casualties soon mounted. One of the M5A1 light tanks attempted to push across the causeway, but hit a mine. This tank, along with a German Hotch-kiss H-39 knocked out in earlier fighting, further congested the narrow passage. Company E tried the crossing next, but along the northern bank

The approaches to Cherbourg were studded with bunkers and other fortifications. This team of GIs from the 79th Division pose near a pillbox they had knocked out with a bazooka during the fighting outside the port. (NARA)

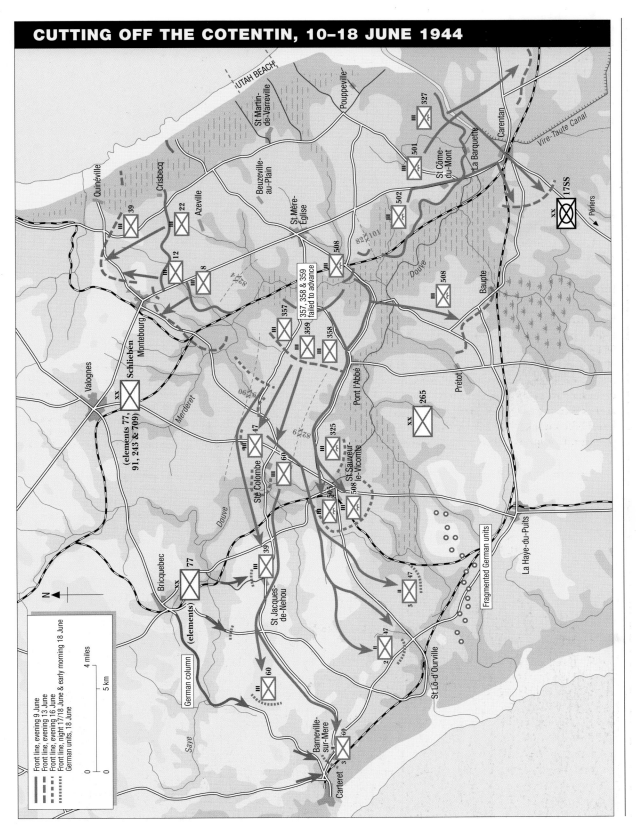

CUTTING OFF THE COTENTIN, 10–18 JUNE 1944

UTAH BEACH

Pouppeville

Carentan

Vire-Taute Canal

327
III
501

St Côme-du-Mont
La Barquette

St Martin-de-Varreville

Beuzeville-au-Plain

502
III

17SS
XX

Péiers

Quinéville

Crisbecq

39
XX

22
III

Azeville

St Mère-Eglise

508
III

Douve

508
III

Baupte

12
III

8
III

824

357
III

359
III
358
III

357, 358 & 359 failed to advance

Pont l'Abbé

265
XX

Prétot

Schlichen
XX
Valognes

(elements 77, 91, 243 & 709)

Montebourg

Merderet

47
III

60
III

325
III

St Sauveur-le-Vicomte
508

Bricquebec

77
XX

Douve

39
III

St Jacques-de-Nehou

47
II
3

Fragmented German units

La Haye-du-Puits

47
II
2

60
III

St Lô-d'Ourville

German column

(elements)

N

Saye

Barneville-sur-Mere
60
Carteret
3

Front line, evening 9 June
Front line, evening 13 June
Front line, evening 16 June
Front line, night 17/18 June & early morning 18 June
German units, 18 June

0   4 miles
0   5 km

A squad of GIs advance through a farm field on the outskirts of Cherbourg. They are probably from the 4th Division as the NCO to the left armed with the M1 carbine is still wearing one of the assault vests issued to combat teams involved in the initial D-Day landings. (NARA)

of the causeway instead of on top of it. They made their way toward the church in Cauquigny, and the German positions were suppressed by small arms fire from Timmes' group. After this company made its way over the bridge and began clearing buildings on the north side of the exit, it was followed by Company F, which pushed beyond the bridgehead toward Le Motey. Due to the usual radio problems, Gavin was unsure of the progress of the 3/325th Glider Infantry and ordered his reserve company from the 507th PIR across the causeway. Further advances westward towards Le Motey were brought to a halt when US artillery continued its fire missions into the area, unaware that US troops had pushed that far. In spite of the many problems, the attacks on 9 June finally cleared the La Fière bridge and causeway.

With passage of the Merderet River open, Collins moved the 90th Division forward to take over the task of moving westward. On 10 June two regiments of the 90th Division began a westward advance over the La Fière and Chef-du-Pont bridges aiming to establish a bridgehead over the Douve River. The 357th Infantry moved over the La Fière bridge but ran into the defenses of GR.1057 past Le Motey. Inexperienced in *bocage* fighting, its lead battalion retreated into the positions of the 325th Glider Infantry. A second attack at dusk by another battalion was equally unsuccessful. The 358th Infantry was assigned to reach Pont l'Abbé, and its lead battalion dug into defense positions short of the objective after coming under heavy fire. GR.1057 launched a counterattack in mid-afternoon, without success.

Infantry advance under the cover of a M4 medium tank of the 740th Tank Battalion during the street fighting inside Cherbourg. (NARA)

The attacks continued the following day with 357th Infantry still unable to overcome the German defensive positions around Les Landes, and the 358th Infantry on the fringe of Pont l'Abbé. The following day, the 359th Infantry rejoined the division from other assignments and reinforced the attack. The 12 June attack was further reinforced by the 746th Tank Battalion and additional artillery fire support. In spite of the reinforcements, the advance on 12 and 13 June was measured in hundreds of yards. In frustration at the slow pace of the advance in four days of fighting, General Collins visited the division on 13 June. After visiting the divisional command post, Collins was aggravated when he could find no regimental or battalion headquarters, nor much evidence of fighting.

Exasperated by the 90th Division's poor performance, Collins telephoned Bradley about his plans to relieve the division's commander and two regimental commanders. He felt that the main problem was the division's poor training and lackluster leadership. They decided to pull the division out of the line in favor of an experienced unit and Bradley agreed to the use of the 9th Division, regarded as being one of the two best

Several Allied warships provided fire support for the Cherbourg operation to deal with the numerous coastal fortifications. Here, the battleship USS *Texas* is the target of a near miss from a German 270mm projectile during the bombardment mission on 25 June 1944. One round hit the *Texas* during the engagement but failed to explode. (NARA)

A pair of M4 medium tanks advance along the battered Rue du Val-de-Saire in the Tourlaville district of Cherbourg on 26 June 1944. The 746th Tank Battalion supported the 9th Division during the fighting in Cherbourg. (NARA)

divisions in theater along with the 1st Division at Omaha Beach. This delayed the advance, so the attack resumed toward the Douve on 15 June with the 82nd Airborne Division on the left and the 9th Division on the right. The 82nd Airborne Division reached St Sauveur on the Douve on 16 June while the 9th Division's 60th Infantry reached the Douve near Ste Colombe. With German resistance crumbling, Collins urged Eddy to push to the sea as rapidly as possible. During the night of 16/17 June, a company from 3/60th Infantry riding on tanks and other armored vehicles reached the hill overlooking the coastal town of Barneville-sur-Mer before dawn. Early in the morning, the company advanced into the town, unoccupied except for a few startled German MPs. The rapid advance by the 9th Division had severed the Cotentin peninsula and cut off Cherbourg.

The sudden isolation of Cherbourg caused a major row among senior German leaders. Rommel had moved the 77th Infantry Division into the Cotentin peninsula on 9 June, but was unwilling to lose the best division in 84th Corps. On 15 June he ordered the amalgamation of the remnants of the 709th Infantry Div. and 243rd Infantry Div. into Kampfgruppe Schlieben with a mission to defend the port of Cherbourg. The 77th Infantry Division, along with the few surviving elements of the 91st Luftlande Division, were formed into Kampfgruppe Hellmich and instructed to withdraw southward if the Americans cut off the peninsula with an aim to prevent any further American penetration south. The capture of St Sauveur prompted Rundstedt and Rommel to begin the withdrawal of Kampfgruppe Schlieben into the Cherbourg area. Rommel and Rundstedt met with Hitler on 16 June at the W2 Battle HQ in Margival, France. Hitler insisted that the largest possible forces be committed to the defense of "Fortress Cherbourg" but he finally agreed to allow Kampfgruppe Hellmich to withdraw southward starting on 17 June. The order proved difficult to implement after both General Hellmich and the commander of the 77th Infantry Division, General Rudolf Stegmann, were killed during air attacks on 17 June. The first unit to begin the withdrawal was GR.1049, which ran into 1/39th Infantry on the morning of 18 June near St Jacques-de-Nehou and was stopped. The neighboring GR.1050 had more success, gaining control of a bridge over the Ollande River near St Lô-d'Ourville from the hapless 357th Infantry of the 90th Division, capturing about 100 GIs and breaking out with about 1,300 men before the gap was finally sealed. In the event, this was the only major group to escape the encirclement, and the 77th Infantry Division lost most of its artillery in the breakout attempt.

NORTH TO CHERBOURG

On 18 June 1944, Field Marshal Bernard Montgomery laid out the immediate tasks for the Allied forces in Normandy. The First US Army was to take Cherbourg while the British Second Army was to take Caen. The breakthrough to the west coast led Bradley to reorganize the forces on the Cotentin peninsula. The new VIII Corps under Major General Troy Middleton was given the 82nd Airborne and 90th Division with an assignment to defend toward the south and prevent any German forces from reinforcing the Cotentin peninsula. Collins' VII Corps now consisted of three infantry divisions, the 4th, 9th and 79th Divisions, which had the mission of advancing on Cherbourg. Eddy's 9th Division began an abrupt change in direction from west to north, moving against the western side of Cherbourg. Barton's 4th Division continued its push up along the eastern coast to Cherbourg, while the newly deployed 79th Division would push up the center. The initial aim was to seize the Quineville ridge, which dominated the terrain southward.

The 4th Division had been fighting northward since D-Day, its advance hampered by the presence of many fortified coastal artillery batteries along the eastern coast. On the left flank, 82nd Airborne's 505th PIR and 4th Division's 8th Infantry Regiment finally reached positions from the Montebourg railroad station to the western outskirts of Montebourg by 11 June. Barton decided against taking the city for fear of tying down too many troops in street fighting. Instead, on 13 June, the 8th Infantry set up defensive positions around the city to contain any German forces within it.

The 22nd Infantry had a much more difficult time, confronting both the Crisbecq and Azeville coastal batteries, which had been reinforced by infantry from the 709th Infantry Division and Sturm.Abt. AOK 7. After repeated attacks, the Azeville position was finally overwhelmed on the afternoon of 9 June by an attack on the command blockhouse with satchel charges and flame-throwers. Frustrated by the failure of previous attacks on Crisbecq, Gen Barton formed Task Force Barber from the 22nd Infantry, reinforced with M10 3in. tank destroyers of the 899th Tank Destroyer Battalion, and tanks of the 746th Tank Battalion. He instructed Barber to skirt around Crisbecq and seize the high ground around

Quineville after taking Ozeville. The attack was frustrated by the thick *bocage*, heavy German artillery fire, and determined counterattacks. The Crisbecq fortifications finally fell on 11 June when 57mm anti-tank guns of K/22nd Infantry fired through the embrasures of the two remaining strongpoints. To gain momentum, Collins took the newly arrived 39th Infantry from the 9th Division and sent it to deal with the many strongpoints along the coast. This freed up Task Force Barber to concentrate on positions further inland, and both air support and naval gunfire support resumed after several days of bad weather. Quineville was finally taken on 14 June, along with the ridgeline to the west, which had been the anchor of German defenses in this sector. Besides clearing the gateway to Cherbourg on the east coast, the operations in the week after D-Day finally ended the threat of German artillery fire into Utah Beach, which had been hampering unloading operations there.

The drive on Cherbourg began on the evening of 19 June with the 4th Division kicking it off at 03.00hrs followed by the 9th and 79th Divisions at 05.00. The 4th Cavalry Group was assigned to protect the right flank of the 4th Division and move up along the eastern coast. German defenses by this stage of the campaign were the disorganized remnants of four divisions. The 9th Division was facing portions of GR.920 and GR.921 from the 243rd Infantry Division along with the surviving elements of the 77th Infantry Division that had failed to escape southward during the breakout attempt two days before. The 79th Division in the center faced parts of the 77th Infantry Division as well as remnants of the 91st Luftlande Division. The 4th Division was facing most of the 709th Infantry Division, the survivors of Sturm.Abt. AOK 7, and large parts of the 243rd Infantry Division.

The initial attacks made steady progress as the German units tended to withdraw after first contact. After the peninsula had been isolated on

17 July, the Cherbourg garrison had been cut off from most outside communication. On 19 July General von Schlieben decided to disengage his forces from the front, and pull them back into a fortified zone on the outskirts of Cherbourg in hopes of conducting a protracted defense. As a result, the American advance only encountered rearguard units or outposts that had lost contact with headquarters. On 20 June Eddy began steps to cut off the Cap de la Hague peninsula from the rest of the Cherbourg defense. German resistance stiffened considerably, and Eddy realized that the 9th Division had finally run into the main line of defense for Fortress Cherbourg.

Von Schlieben reorganized his disparate forces into four battle-groups (*kampfgruppe*) that formed a semicircular defensive line outside the city. The German defenses were based on a series of hills and ridges located four to six miles from the port. Many of the defenses included bunkers, while others included concrete structures of the abandoned V-1 buzz bomb bases. The attack on Cherbourg was preceded by an intense air preparation conducted by the IX Tactical Air Command. The ground attack on the afternoon of 22 June was preceded at 12.40hrs by 25 minutes of rocket attacks and strafing by ten squadrons of Typhoons and Mustangs of the 2nd Tactical Air Force (RAF), 55 minutes of bombing and strafing by 562 P-47s and P-51s, followed at H-Hour (14.00) by bombing runs of 11 groups of B-26 Marauders of the Ninth Air Force. The air attacks proved

A group of GIs and French civilians celebrate the capture of Cherbourg, driving around the city in a captured Renault UE tractor. (NARA)

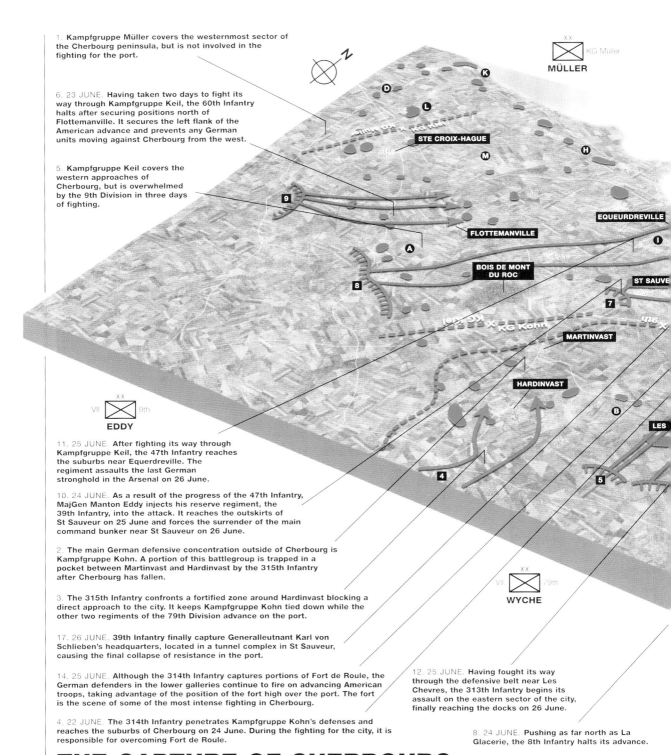

1. Kampfgruppe Müller covers the westernmost sector of the Cherbourg peninsula, but is not involved in the fighting for the port.

6. 23 JUNE. Having taken two days to fight its way through Kampfgruppe Keil, the 60th Infantry halts after securing positions north of Flottemanville. It secures the left flank of the American advance and prevents any German units moving against Cherbourg from the west.

5. Kampfgruppe Keil covers the western approaches of Cherbourg, but is overwhelmed by the 9th Division in three days of fighting.

XX
KG Muller
MÜLLER

K
D
L
STE CROIX-HAGUE
M
H

9

EQUEURDREVILLE

A
FLOTTEMANVILLE
I

BOIS DE MONT DU ROC
ST SAUVE

8
7

KG Kohn
MARTINVAST

HARDINVAST

B
LES

XX
VII   9th
EDDY

11. 25 JUNE. After fighting its way through Kampfgruppe Keil, the 47th Infantry reaches the suburbs near Equerdreville. The regiment assaults the last German stronghold in the Arsenal on 26 June.

10. 24 JUNE. As a result of the progress of the 47th Infantry, MajGen Manton Eddy injects his reserve regiment, the 39th Infantry, into the attack. It reaches the outskirts of St Sauveur on 25 June and forces the surrender of the main command bunker near St Sauveur on 26 June.

2. The main German defensive concentration outside of Cherbourg is Kampfgruppe Kohn. A portion of this battlegroup is trapped in a pocket between Martinvast and Hardinvast by the 315th Infantry after Cherbourg has fallen.

3. The 315th Infantry confronts a fortified zone around Hardinvast blocking a direct approach to the city. It keeps Kampfgruppe Kohn tied down while the other two regiments of the 79th Division advance on the port.

17. 26 JUNE. 39th Infantry finally capture Generalleutnant Karl von Schlieben's headquarters, located in a tunnel complex in St Sauveur, causing the final collapse of resistance in the port.

14. 25 JUNE. Although the 314th Infantry captures portions of Fort de Roule, the German defenders in the lower galleries continue to fire on advancing American troops, taking advantage of the position of the fort high over the port. The fort is the scene of some of the most intense fighting in Cherbourg.

4. 22 JUNE. The 314th Infantry penetrates Kampfgruppe Kohn's defenses and reaches the suburbs of Cherbourg on 24 June. During the fighting for the city, it is responsible for overcoming Fort de Roule.

4

5

XX
VII   79th
WYCHE

12. 25 JUNE. Having fought its way through the defensive belt near Les Chevres, the 313th Infantry begins its assault on the eastern sector of the city, finally reaching the docks on 26 June.

8. 24 JUNE. Pushing as far north as La Glacerie, the 8th Infantry halts its advance.

THE CAPTURE OF CHERBOURG

22–30 June 1944, viewed from the southeast, showing the assault on this vital strategic port by US 4th, 9th, and 79th Infantry Divisions. The city was captured amid bitter fighting, but comprehensive destruction of facilities by the German defenders rendered the port of Cherbourg useless to the Allies for many weeks.

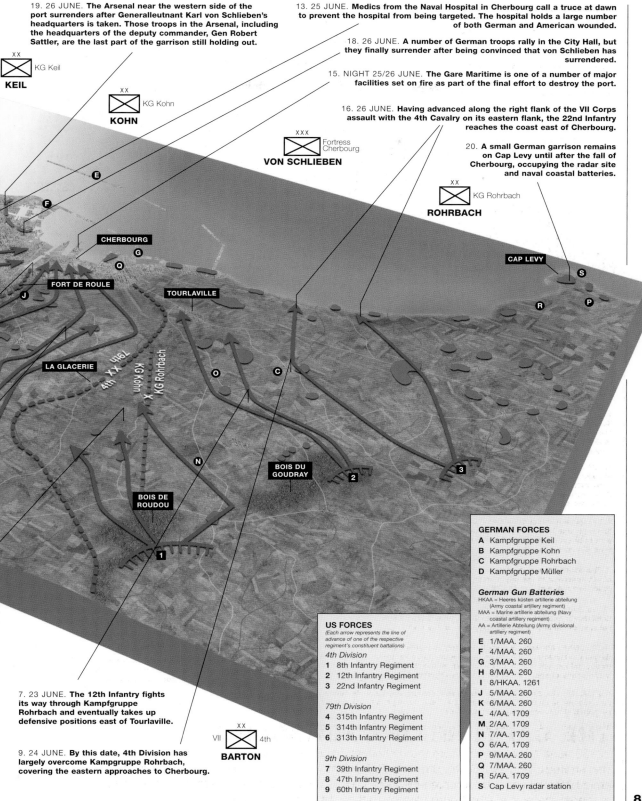

19. 26 JUNE. The Arsenal near the western side of the port surrenders after Generalleutnant Karl von Schlieben's headquarters is taken. Those troops in the Arsenal, including the headquarters of the deputy commander, Gen Robert Sattler, are the last part of the garrison still holding out.

13. 25 JUNE. Medics from the Naval Hospital in Cherbourg call a truce at dawn to prevent the hospital from being targeted. The hospital holds a large number of both German and American wounded.

18. 26 JUNE. A number of German troops rally in the City Hall, but they finally surrender after being convinced that von Schlieben has surrendered.

15. NIGHT 25/26 JUNE. The Gare Maritime is one of a number of major facilities set on fire as part of the final effort to destroy the port.

16. 26 JUNE. Having advanced along the right flank of the VII Corps assault with the 4th Cavalry on its eastern flank, the 22nd Infantry reaches the coast east of Cherbourg.

20. A small German garrison remains on Cap Levy until after the fall of Cherbourg, occupying the radar site and naval coastal batteries.

KG Keil
KEIL

KG Kohn
KOHN

Fortress Cherbourg
VON SCHLIEBEN

KG Rohrbach
ROHRBACH

E
F
CHERBOURG
G
Q
FORT DE ROULE
J
TOURLAVILLE
LA GLACERIE
79th
4th
KG Kohn
KG Rohrbach
O
C
N
BOIS DU GOUDRAY
2
3
BOIS DE ROUDOU
1
CAP LEVY
S
R
P

7. 23 JUNE. The 12th Infantry fights its way through Kampfgruppe Rohrbach and eventually takes up defensive positions east of Tourlaville.

9. 24 JUNE. By this date, 4th Division has largely overcome Kampfgruppe Rohrbach, covering the eastern approaches to Cherbourg.

VII   4th
BARTON

GERMAN FORCES
A Kampfgruppe Keil
B Kampfgruppe Kohn
C Kampfgruppe Rohrbach
D Kampfgruppe Müller

German Gun Batteries
HKAA = Heeres küsten artillerie abteilung (Army coastal artillery regiment)
MAA = Marine artillerie abteilung (Navy coastal artillery regiment)
AA = Artillerie Abteilung (Army divisional artillery regiment)
E 1/MAA. 260
F 4/MAA. 260
G 3/MAA. 260
H 8/MAA. 260
I 8/HKAA. 1261
J 5/MAA. 260
K 6/MAA. 260
L 4/AA. 1709
M 2/AA. 1709
N 7/AA. 1709
O 6/AA. 1709
P 9/MAA. 260
Q 7/MAA. 260
R 5/AA. 1709
S Cap Levy radar station

US FORCES
(Each arrow represents the line of advance of one of the respective regiment's constituent battalions)
4th Division
1 8th Infantry Regiment
2 12th Infantry Regiment
3 22nd Infantry Regiment

79th Division
4 315th Infantry Regiment
5 314th Infantry Regiment
6 313th Infantry Regiment

9th Division
7 39th Infantry Regiment
8 47th Infantry Regiment
9 60th Infantry Regiment

less effective than anticipated, and many infantry units radioed that they were being inadvertently attacked. The best results had been obtained on the western side where the 9th Division artillery had suppressed German flak positions in anticipation of the air missions. None of the main defenses were cracked on 22 June, and it took two days of hard fighting before the first portions of the defensive belt were finally overcome. The first penetrations past the outer defenses took place in the 9th Division's sector near the Flottemanville–Hague strongpoints late in the evening of 23 June.

Although von Schlieben was in command of the four divisions holding the city, the actual command of the port was under Generalmajor Robert Sattler until 23 June when Hitler appointed von Schlieben as the commander of Fortress Cherbourg. Requests for further ammunition and reinforcements went unanswered, but senior German commanders felt that the garrison could hold out for months due to the geography and the extensive fortifications around the port.

The final assaults into the town were made by infantry–tank teams, with each of the divisions receiving a separate tank battalion for support. These were essential to deal with the many bunkers and defenses encountered. Although German resistance on 24 June continued to be intense, there was a growing tendency for the defenses to crumble once vigorously assaulted. By the end of the day, breaches had been made in the final layer of outer defenses, allowing the first access to the city itself. At dawn on 25 June, a German medical officer accompanied by a captured American pilot came out under a flag of truce to ask that the naval hospital be spared from shelling and for a supply of plasma. They were allowed to return to the city with the plasma, and with a demand for the immediate surrender of the city. By the time the demand had reached von Schlieben, the 314th Infantry was already assaulting Fort de Roule overlooking the city. The intensity of the fighting for the fort is evident from the fact that two Medals of Honor for bravery were awarded for the action. By midnight, the 314th Infantry had broken into the fort and occupied the upper levels, but with German troops still occupying the lower galleries. The 47th Infantry made the first penetration into the suburbs of Cherbourg on 25 June after overcoming the defenses at Equeurdreville. By nightfall the city was illuminated by the fires of the burning port facilities that the Germans had set as the final stage of the destruction of the port.

The final assault into the city by the 9th and 79th Division occurred on 26 June. US patrols in the city continued to be harassed by artillery fire from the lower levels of Fort de Roule, which were still in German hands. These lower levels were not immediately accessible to the troops from 2/314th Infantry on top of the fort, and they began to try to lower charges down ventilation shafts. A demolition team snaked its way along the cliff face on the western side of the fort and blasted one of the tunnel openings with pole charges and bazookas. Troops below the fort began firing into the embrasures with 57mm anti-tank guns. Resistance finally collapsed in the early evening and several hundred prisoners were taken.

Fighting in the city remained intense through the day, and the presence of many large concrete structures and coastal gun positions greatly complicated the American attacks. The 39th Infantry learned from prisoners that Gen Schlieben was in a bunker in St Sauveur, and by mid-afternoon Companies E and F had fought their way to the tunnel entrance of the command bunker. A prisoner was sent in to demand surrender, which was refused. M10 tank destroyers were brought forward, and a few 3in. high explosive rounds were enough to cause the Germans to reconsider. About 800 officers and troops began to pour out including General von Schlieben, Admiral Walter Hennecke, and their staffs. The surrender was made to Gen Eddy, but von Schlieben refused to order the surrender of the rest of his garrison. Nevertheless, the forces still holding the City Hall surrendered after learning of von Schlieben's surrender. The last major defensive position in the city was the Arsenal, which was protected by a moat and strongly defended by anti-aircraft and anti-tank guns on parapets. The 47th Infantry was assigned to take it on the morning of 26 June, and began by picking off two of the 20mm Flak parapets with tank fire. Before the main assault at 08.30hrs, a psychological warfare unit brought up a loudspeaker, urging the garrison to surrender. General Sattler, the deputy commander of Cherbourg, agreed to surrender the 400 men under his command, and the rest of the arsenal surrendered by 10.00hrs. This ended the organized resistance in the port, though mopping-up operations continued for two days. About 10,000 prisoners were captured on 25–26 June. Two more days were spent eliminating outlying forts in the harbor, mainly by air attack and tank gun fire. There were also isolated garrisons on Cap Levy that were taken by the 22nd Infantry, and about 3,000 Germans had retreated to Cap de la Hague. The 9th Division assaulted these positions and overran the final defenses on 30 June. A total of 6,000 prisoners were captured in the final operations in late June. On 1 July, the 9th Division reported to Collins that all organized resistance on the Cotentin peninsula had ended.

The total casualties of the VII Corps from D-Day to the fall of Cherbourg at the end of June was about 22,000. The large number of missing was due to scattered airborne landings that accounted for 4,500 of the missing, some of whom were captured. German casualties are not known with any precision although prisoners totaled 39,000. The allies had hoped to capture Cherbourg by D+15, so its capture on D+21 was not far behind schedule, especially compared to the plans for Caen in the neighboring British sector. The capture of Cherbourg did not provide any immediate benefit to the Allied supply situation, as the Germans had thoroughly demolished the port facilities prior to the surrender. Their one failure in this regard was the large fuel storage facility in the port, which remained intact and quite valuable to the Allies. It took almost two months to clean up the port, but it was back in operation by September 1944.

Table 3: US VII Corps Casualties D-Day to 1 July 1944

Unit	killed	wounded	missing	captured	Total
4th Div.	844	3,814	788	6	5,452
9th Div.	301	2,061	76		2,438
79th Div.	240	1,896	240		2,376
90th Div.	386	1,979	34		2,399
82nd Abn. Div.	457	1,440	2,571	12+	4,480
101st Abn. Div	546	2,217	1,907	?	4,670
Corps troops	37	157	49	61	304
Total	2,811	13,564	5,665	79	22,119

The fall of the port shocked Hitler and the senior German leadership who believed that such a heavily fortified facility could hold out for months. They seriously overestimated the paper strength of their own forces and seriously underestimated combat efficiency of the US Army. With the capture of the Cotentin peninsula, hope evaporated that the Allies could be dislodged from France.

THE BATTLEFIELD TODAY

In contrast to Omaha Beach, where most of the combat action occurred on the beach itself, the fighting for Utah Beach was over very quickly. The most intense D-Day fighting in this sector consisted of small skirmishes by the paratroopers scattered in the farmland behind the beach. There is a museum near the beach itself, and a significant number of German fortifications remain, including some preserved artillery emplacements. The "Musee de Debarquement d'Utah Beach" is located in Ste Marie-du-Mont adjacent to the beach and includes many exhibits of weapons and equipment associated with the landing. The area behind the beach that was flooded at the time of D-Day has long since been drained and is now farmland.

Of all the sites connected with the paratrooper actions, Ste Mère-Église is no doubt the most popular, due in no small measure to the dramatic depiction in the well-known film "The Longest Day". None other than John Wayne depicted (the much younger!) LtCol Benjamin Vandervoort. The images of Red Buttons in the film, depicting Pvt John Steele hanging by his parachute from the church steeple, is one of the most memorable in the movie. For years, the church in Ste Mère-Église has had a mannequin hanging from a parachute draped from the roof to commemorate the airborne landings. The church also contains a stained glass window commemorating the 505th PIR, which was added on the 25th anniversary. There is a large museum in the town, the "Musee des Troupe Aeroportees", devoted to the airborne landings.

This picture of Utah Beach was taken in 1947, and the area is very similar today. Compared to the photo on p.53, which shows the beach on D-Day, the flooded areas behind the beach have been drained and returned to use as farmland. (MHI)

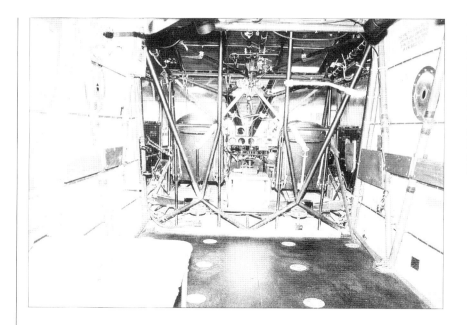

The 82nd Airborne Division Museum at Ft. Bragg has preserved one of the few surviving Waco CG-4A gliders. In spite of their canvas covering, their tubular fuselage construction proved to be relatively robust for such a light airframe. The canvas bench seat for the glider infantry can be seen in the left foreground. (Author)

The countryside around Ste Mère-Église is dotted with dozens of small markers, monuments, shrines, and plaques. Some of these are memorials to various units that took part in the fighting, while some commemorate individuals, such as a plaque at the site where General Pratt was killed. It is helpful to have a guidebook or map to seek out these memorials, as many are remote from the main roads. La Fière bridge still exists, though it is still as inconspicuous as in 1944. Nearby is the famous "Iron Mike" monument to the paratroopers. There are markers nearby showing the depth of the water of the flooded farm fields, but it takes some imagination to recall how difficult the fight along the causeway must have been.

The numerous concrete fortifications erected by the Germans along the coast in many cases still exist, as the larger bunkers are so difficult and costly to remove. Many of these are on private land, and tourists should take extreme care when visiting such sites as many contain sub-basements that present a real hazard to the unprepared. Some of the most impressive fortifications are the Crisbecq and Azeville batteries and there is a museum (La Batterie d'Azeville) open in the summer months nearby. Cherbourg has been heavily rebuilt since the war, and the Fort de Roule has been converted into the "Musee de la Liberation".

American servicemen killed in action were interred in the American Cemetery and Memorial, located in Colleville-sur-Mer near the St Laurent draw on Omaha Beach. There are two German military cemeteries near Utah Beach, the Orglandes cemetery about seven miles from Ste Mère-Église and the larger cemetery at La Cambe, which is about 17 miles southeast of Ste Mère-Église.

FURTHER READING

The D-Day landings are one of the most popular topics of World War II history, and there are hundreds of titles on this subject of varying quality. There was a flood of new books around the time of the 1994 anniversary. Paratroop operations are of particular fascination to many military history buffs, and many surveys of airborne operations cover the D-Day jumps. The list below is by no means exhaustive and consists mainly of more recent titles that the author has found to be particularly useful. Besides the commercially published books, there are a number of limited-circulation books by US Army commands that are particularly useful for those looking for more in-depth coverage, and they can be found in specialist military libraries. In contrast to the V Corps history covering Omaha Beach, the VII Corps history is weak and not worth the effort to locate. Of the semi-official divisional histories, several have been reprinted by Battery Press, including the 9th, 79th, and 101st Airborne. The multi-volume 4th Division History has not been reprinted, but is not as detailed as other divisional histories dealing with D-Day. There are also many after-action reports on the D-Day landings that are more difficult to find except at archives. The author consulted the collections at the Military History Institute at the Army War College at Carlisle Barracks, Pennsylvania, and the US National Archives and Records Administration (NARA) at College Park, Maryland. One of the most useful studies is USAF Historical Study No. 97, prepared at the Air University in 1957, entitled "Airborne Operations in World War II: European Theater", which provides an excellent account and pointed critique of the conduct of the D-Day airborne landings. There are also numerous after-action reports by the various US Army units located in Record Group 407 at NARA, College Park. There have been a number of films devoted to D-Day, including Darryl Zanuck's memorable epic "The Longest Day", which devotes considerable time to the airborne landings around Ste Mère-Église. A more contemporary depiction of the airborne operations is included in Steven Spielberg's multi-part TV-movie "Band of Brothers" based on the excellent Stephen Ambrose book about a company of the 101st Airborne.

Ambrose, Stephen, *D-Day, June 6, 1944* (Simon & Schuster, 1994). This account of the D-Day landings by the popular historian is based on many interviews with veterans that presents the soldiers' perspectives of the fighting.

Bando, Mark, *101st Airborne: The Screaming Eagles at Normandy* (MBI, 2001). This is an excellent photographic portrait of the 101st Airborne in Normandy with many detailed accounts of individual actions based on interviews with veterans.

Bernage, George, *Debarquement à Utah Beach* (Heimdal, 1984). This short but useful photographic portrayal of Utah Beach on D-Day has excellent details on the German beach defenses.

Bernage, George, *Premiere Victoire Americaine en Normandie* (Heimdal, 1990). Another useful Heimdal photo book by this prolific French specialist on Normandy; this time covering the battle for Cherbourg.

Collins, J. Lawton, *Lightning Joe* (LSU Press, 1979). An excellent autobiography by the VII Corps commander with insightful comments about the conduct of the fighting.

Esvelin, Philippe, D-Day Gliders, *Les planeurs Americains du Jour J* (Heimdal, 2002). A short and excellent photographic account of the glider operations on D-Day.

Gawne, Jonathan, *Spearheading D-Day* (Histoire & Collections, 1998). A superb and lavishly illustrated examination of the US special units deployed during the Normandy landings with excellent coverage of their equipment and uniforms.

Harrison, Gordon, *Cross-Channel Attack* (US Army CMH, 1951). This is the official US Army "Green Book" history of the Normandy landings and remains one of the best available accounts.

Isby, David, *Fighting the Invasion: The German Army at D-Day* (Greenhill, 2000). This is the best single volume on the German army on D-Day and consists of a collection of essays written by senior German leaders for the US Army's Foreign Military Studies program after the war based on their recollections of the campaign.

Isby, David, *Fighting the Invasion: The German Army from D-Day to Villers Bocage* (Greenhill, 2001). This is a follow-on to the first volume and takes the action into mid-June. It has good coverage of several of the German units prominent in the Cotentin peninsula fighting, especially FJR 6 and the 709th Infantry Division.

Koskimaki, George, *D-Day with the Screaming Eagles* (1970, Casemate reprint 2002). A classic by Gen Taylor's radioman, who has collected a wealth of fellow veterans accounts.

Masters, Charles J., *Glidermen of Neptune* (S. Illinois University Press, 1995). An account of the glider operations on D-Day by the son of one of the glider infantrymen.

Morison, Samuel E., *The Invasion of France and Germany 1944–1945* (Little, Brown, 1957). This volume of Morison's history of the US Navy in World War II remains the best single account of US Navy actions on D-Day.

Ramsey, Winston, *D-Day Then and Now, Volume 2* (After the Battle, 1995). This is a typically lavish and massive "After the Battle" treatment with an excellent selection of historical photos, complemented by photos of the same sites today.

Rapaport, Leonard, Northwood, A., *Rendezvous with Destiny* (Infantry Journal; Battery Press Reprint). A classic divisional history of the 101st Airborne and one of the best studies of a US WWII division.

Shilleto, Carl, *Utah Beach: Ste Mère-Église* (Leo Cooper, 2001). This is one of the popular Battleground Europe paperbacks combining a tour guide of the battlefield with a short narrative of the battle.

Utah Beach to Cherbourg (US Army Center for Military History, 1946; many reprints). This short account of Utah Beach preceded the "green book" history but still remains valuable.

Wolfe, Martin, *Green Light: A Troop Carrier Squadron's War from Normandy to the Rhine* (Univ. Of Pennsylvania Press, 1983). An account of the Normandy airdrops from the perspective of one of the C-47 pilots provides an interesting contrast to the paratrooper accounts which are often critical of the transport pilots.

INDEX